Viktor Frankl and
the Psychology of the Soul

Viktor Frankl

and the

Psychology of the Soul

A GUIDE TO FINDING MEANING AND EMOTIONAL WELLNESS

By Rabbi Daniel Schonbuch, LMFT

ISBN: 979-8-9912084-0-6 Trade Paperback
ISBN: 979-8-9912084-1-3 eBook

Library of Congress Control Number: 00000000000

Cover photo by permission of Brandstaetter Images
Book design by Glen Edelstein, Hudson Valley Book Design

Printed by IngramSpark, in the United States of America.

First printing edition 2024

Contents

Dedication

This book is dedicated to my grandmother, Frances (Fayge Mariasha) Aron, who taught me the remarkable balance between wisdom and kindness.

It was written in honor of *Shnas Hakhel*, 5783.

"I particularly took interest in the writing of Dr. Frankl (from Vienna) in this matter. To my surprise, however, his approach has apparently not been appropriately disseminated and appreciated."[1]

—Rabbi Menachem Mendel Schneersohn, the Lubavitcher Rebbe

Introduction

If you lack meaning in your life—or if you suffer from depression, anxiety, or trauma—you may wonder if undergoing significant psychotherapy, spending years focusing on your childhood or exploring your traumatic history, is your only option. For over a century, the practice of psychotherapy has focused on exploring your painful memories, negative beliefs, or distorted thinking patterns, but *not* on your desire to find meaning in your life.

Viktor Frankl's psychology called logotherapy (the therapy of meaning) takes a different direction. He was an eminent psychiatrist and neurologist who challenged the very foundations of psychotherapy. In two of his seminal books, *Man's Search for Meaning* and *The Unconscious God*, Frankl maintained that a person's most basic need is to find meaning. When this need is frustrated and a person can't find anything to live for, the "existential vacuum" leads to feelings of depression and anxiety.

Frankl's approach is significantly different from that of Sigmund Freud, Alfred Adler and many other well-known therapists. Unlike psychoanalysis or individual psychology that dig deeply into one's childhood and focus on overcoming negative aspects of the "self," Frankl maintained that too much self-focus may actually *worsen* your symptoms. Logotherapy therefore helps a person to go beyond the "self"—search for meaning—and access their higher spiritual strengths. Frankl believed that instead of going deeper into a person's past, they need to go higher.

Logotherapy is built on three main concepts:

- Freedom of Will—We are free to make choices and take a stand.
- The Will to Meaning—Our primary search in life is for finding meaning.
- The Meaning of Life—We can find meaning, even in the most difficult situations.

These concepts will be explored throughout the book as I take the reader on a journey into finding and actualizing more meaning in life. As you follow these steps, you will learn how to focus beyond yourself, uncover your latent spiritual resources, and start feeling better.

Spiritual Integration

Logotherapy doesn't stand alone. Frankl believed that "[Logotherapy] is open to cooperation with other scientifically established psychotherapies, and open to its own evolution, to the full development of its potential."[2] As a rabbi and therapist I have taken his lead and augmented Frankl's ideas presented in *The Unconscious God* by incorporating Logotherapy within a psycho-spiritual approach enriched by the teachings of Rabbi Dovber Shneuri, also known as the Mitteler Rebbe.

The Mitteler Rebbe was a spiritual giant whose unique writings uncovered both the method of spiritual contemplation and the effects that occur by focusing beyond yourself and on God's existence. He provided a framework on how to actualize what Frankl refers to as the "unconscious God" (see chapter 5).

Although they never met, they were both descendants of the Maharal of Prague, Rabbi Judah Loew ben Bezalel, a 16th Century Talmudic scholar, kabbalist, mathematician, astronomer, and philosopher. I maintain that the Mitteler Rebbe's ideas greatly enrich the spiritual components of Logotherapy outlined by Frankl and will add to the reader's experience in finding meaning in their lives.

A New Approach

Now, you may be skeptical of yet another new type of therapy given the proliferation of novel practices claiming to solve any and all of one's issues. I am aware of the many new types of therapy that are being practiced today and what they believe they can achieve. I have trained in and utilize a wide array of techniques such as Cognitive Behavioral Therapy (CBT), Eye Movement Desensitization and Reprocessing (EMDR), Somatic Experiencing, and Internal Family Systems (IFS).

During my years of training and practice with thousands of clients, I have learned that each psychological technique comes with its strengths and weaknesses. However, nothing I have seen is as powerful in rapidly unlocking the emotional healing powers as those of logotherapy. When you focus on goodness and spirituality within a psychological framework, remarkable things happen in therapy—and very quickly.

Searching for Meaning as Human Nature

Throughout this book, you'll see how (without even knowing) many people intuitively access higher levels of meaning or unconscious Godliness, and by doing so, they transform their lives. Through the heroic lives of people like Rabbi Yitzi Hurwitz, who struggles with ALS; Jerry Long, a paraplegic who became a psychotherapist; Viktor Frankl, who survived Auschwitz and became one of the most prolific writers of the twentieth century; Vanessa, a woman who broke her neck and became an inspiration to countless others who are dealing with inescapable suffering; Rivkah, who lost her baby in a stillbirth; and Sara, who fights a courageous battle against AS (Ankylosing Spondylitis), a debilitating autoimmune disease, the book will help you find your true self and your purpose in life, and you'll be helped to experience emotional healing and well-being.

Ten Levels of Meaning

You will also learn about the Ten Levels of Meaning (see diagram below) that are an emotional GPS guiding you to uncover new emotional resources based on your values, your spirituality, and your relationship with God. These Ten Levels will assist you in understanding the meaning behind what you are thinking and feeling and will help you move from a more limited view of yourself to an expanded and far-reaching perception of what you can accomplish on the road to living a meaningful life.

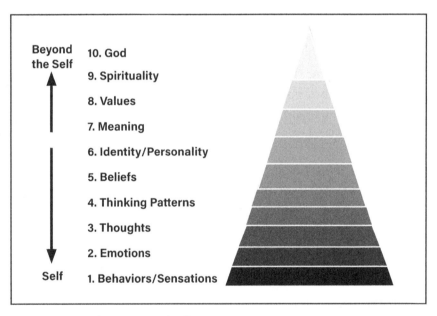

Beyond the Self

10. God

9. Spirituality

8. Values

7. Meaning

6. Identity/Personality

5. Beliefs

4. Thinking Patterns

3. Thoughts

2. Emotions

Self

1. Behaviors/Sensations

The Search for Meaning 30-Day Logotherapy Workbook

For those looking to experience the power of Logotherapy, I created a workbook which readers can find at the end of this book. By following the exercises in the "Search for Meaning 30-Day Logotherapy Workbook" and by journalling for just a few minutes per day, I believe you will witness significant emotional changes in your life.

CHAPTER 1:

How the Search for Meaning Heals Depression, Anxiety, and PTSD

"There is nothing in the world, I venture to say, that would so effectively help one to survive even the worst conditions as the knowledge that there is a meaning in one's life."
—**Viktor E. Frankl,** *Man's Search for Meaning*

I s there a secret psychological technique that can help people find meaning and overcome depression, anxiety, or the long-term effects of trauma? Since the time of Sigmund Freud, modern psychology has maintained that you must spend significant time revisiting your childhood or reliving and desensitizing yourself to your past traumas. But is that true?

Rabbi Yitzi Hurwitz may have the answer. He props his head up on his bed so he can see his friends and family. Since he can't breathe on his own, he's attached to a respirator. As a result of Lou Gehrig's disease, he can't move. However, by using his eyes, he communicates with his wife, kids, and thousands around the world who read his heartfelt thoughts on the weekly Torah portion.

Each day he uses computer assisted technology to communicate with the world, despite how unbelievably painstaking it is to communicate even one letter. Many of us have been inspired by Rabbi Hurwitz, especially those who have trouble finding light in their emotional darkness.

The circumstances facing Yitzi Hurwitz would overwhelm most people and incapacitate them. How does he persevere? How does he tap into his authentic spirituality and goodness and find meaning? He certainly didn't learn it from a psychology textbook and probably didn't read about it in a self-help book. So, how does he sidestep despair and continue to inspire people around the world?

Man's Search for Meaning

Viktor Frankl addresses this question in his epic work, *Man's Search for Meaning*. As a psychiatrist and survivor of Auschwitz, there is no better person for the job. Frankl pioneered Logotherapy, or the psychology of meaning, which maintains that human action is driven, above all else by our search for purpose. And tapping into this drive unleashes remarkable powers of emotional healing and transformation.

Frankl explained how he utilized his "will to meaning" in Auschwitz when there were no options left to him and the other prisoners. Don't forget, his situation was desperate. The Nazis barely fed them, they were subjected to daily beatings, and many were sent to the crematoria for extermination. The only freedom left existed within his mind, and he could choose to change his attitude or find meaning in other areas of his existence.

Finding meaning may have meant sharing a good word with another prisoner or giving him a morsel of his bread. When that was not possible, the only option left was to change one's attitude. Some chose to sanctify one's life for God "al *Kiddush Hashem*" with the words *Shema Yisrael* uttered before their death, or they would think about fulfilling a meaningful goal in the future.

At times, Frankl imagined being reunited and talking with his wife after the war (even though he didn't know if she had already died in Auschwitz). This, he claimed, was what differentiated those who lost hope from those who still aimed to live, the fulfillment of a sense of meaning whether big or small.

As Frankl said, "In the Nazi concentration camps, one could have witnessed that those who knew that there was a task waiting for them to fulfill were most apt to survive." According to Frankl, if we could peel back the layers of a person's mind to find the fundamental core of what makes us human—and what keeps us alive—we would discover that our most basic drive is not for pleasure (as proposed by Freud), nor power (as suggested by Alfred Adler), nor is it due to our cognitive distortions (Beck), but the will to live a life with meaning.

The will to meaning turns out to be the most essential force within us that keeps us alive, even when all else is taken away from us. And it is this "will" that we must follow to achieve emotional well-being.

My own experience of childhood trauma, related to my father's devastating accident, led me to read Frankl's books as a young adult, and the results lasted a lifetime. Frankl's ideas left an indelible impression on me and shaped my career choices. As a therapist, his teachings inspired me to help my clients in discovering meaning in their work, relationships, or even in the face of inescapable circumstances such as losing loved ones or suffering chronic illness.

Meditative Moment. What meaning do you long to fulfill? Is there an experience, value, or idea that has already helped you change your life? How would finding more meaning give your life more direction right now?

The Unconscious God

Where does this drive for meaning exist in human consciousness? Frankl identified the source in a lesser-known book called, *The Unconscious God*, where he describes the psychological unconscious goodness and "will" for spirituality and God.

According to Frankl, this part of our unconscious mind is called the *religio*, which guides us in discovering our spiritual nature and connecting with God.[1] Frankl used this term to imply that God remains hidden in the unconscious, meaning that one's relationship with Him is unknown to oneself. However, when this will is brought into a person's consciousness, it can guide the person to overcome any emotional challenges they are facing.

Frankl spoke extensively about these hidden spiritual and religious desires in a period that was dominated by the teachings of Sigmund Freud. It was Freud, the father of psychoanalysis, who dominated psycho-therapy for over half a century. He maintained a decidedly negative attitude towards spirituality and God. He believed that God was a human invention created to reduce fears of helplessness.[2] Freud therefore dissuaded his clients from seeking spiritual endeavors, insisting that they were merely a crutch people leaned on to manage their fears.

Frankl took a decidedly different approach. He believed that following the unconscious drive for meaning and for God (the religio), was the cure for man's psychological dilemmas. Logotherapy therefore provides a framework to find the internal "spark" needed for change. In a session, this takes on many different avenues including helping the client discover their creativity, fulfilling their values, finding someone to love, or fulfilling some lifelong dream or task. We operate under the premise that everyone has a deep reservoir of hidden spiritual strengths and emotional resources waiting to be brought into consciousness.

Focusing on discovering meaning and uncovering the inner will for spirituality kindles a remarkable type of emotional transformation. When my clients identify this "spark" they often report feeling a new type of "wholeness" accompanied by feelings of euphoria or joy. And, it is these kinds of positive emotions that are necessary to battle depression, anxiety, or post-traumatic stress disorder.

Instead of dredging up and focusing on negative emotions, Logotherapy arouses powerful emotional resources that literally shift the individual into a positive and forward-thinking mindset. This new mindset becomes the catalyst towards emotional change and personal resilience.

Meditative Moment. Think about your mistakes in life for a moment. Then, pay attention to your inner spark of creativity or your drive to find meaning in life. Which helps you more: thinking about your mistakes and failures, or focusing on your inner spark for meaning?

Rabbi Dovber, the Mitteler Rebbe

As a rabbi and therapist, I also expand the key spiritual concepts outlined in *The Unconscious God* with the ideas of Rabbi Dovber Shneuri, also known as the Mitteler Rebbe (1773–1827). Rabbi Dovber articulated a system of contemplative meditation that forms the basis of spiritually-based psychology.

Two of his seminal treatises, the "*Tract on Contemplation*" and the "*Tract on Ecstasy,*" offer a detailed and comprehensive method of analysis and observation. Similar to what Frankl is alluding to, Rabbi Dovber describes the psycho-spiritual power of the Godly soul and what happens to a person when they think about God. I utilize this approach in helping my clients grow from a psychological perspective.

The ideas of both Rabbi Dovber and Viktor Frankl exist in great contradistinction to classical schools of psychology, where the goals are to help patients resolve inner conflicts, deal with childhood traumas, or change their negative self-beliefs.

If we look at the real needs of most of our clients, it is apparent that psychotherapy that only explores people's pasts only offers one dimension to resolving their emotional problems. Additionally, the cost of extensive psychotherapy creates certain limitations. How can meeting with a therapist once a week for forty-five minutes provide enough support for our clients to grow?

The therapeutic methods of Dr. Margaret Wehrenberg, a nationally recognized psychologist who specializes in treating depression, concurs with the approach offered by Frankl. She explains how therapy needs to be augmented with daily spirit habits:

> Evidence continues to accumulate that many people who have anxiety and depression suffer bouts of it all their lives, even after a good response to therapy. Therapists need to provide individualized care and tools (including social support) to cope with unexpected changes, along with a daily program of meditation

and spiritual connection, and daily optimistic reminders of the chronicity of their condition and how they're managing it.[3]

According to Wehrenberg, it's not just about the 45-minute weekly sessions with our clients that create healing, but the spiritual habits that we help our clients develop. Talk therapy is the Band-Aid, whereas Logotherapy is akin to stitches. When a client discovers their internal spiritual resources, these spiritual desires now lead the person towards constant emotional growth, long after they leave the therapist's office.

Like Wehrenberg, I have met with many clients suffering from depression and anxiety who felt therapy was unable to fully heal their pain. After years of sitting on the "couch," many were still struggling with persistent feelings of worry or sadness. They needed more than traditional talk therapy to feel better. The frustration these clients experienced as they tried various therapies, without feeling lasting results, challenged me to create a comprehensive approach and a method towards combating depression and anxiety.

Meditative Moment. What are your spiritual rituals or practices that bring you strength and hope? Are you aware of them on a daily level? Which spiritual practices could you incorporate in your daily life that would change how you feel?

Finding a Framework

How does one utilize the teachings of Frankl and Rabbi Dovber to heal their emotional pain? For therapists and the public alike, there is very little practical instruction on how to incorporate Viktor Frankl's Logotherapy and the writings of Rabbi Dovber into one's practice. This may be due to the philosophical nature of Frankl's writings or the complexity of Rabbi Dovber's writings.

Over the past decade, I have developed a psycho-spiritual system of psychology which can be accessed by therapists and clients alike. Some of that work is described in my previous book, *Think Good and It Will Be Good.*[4]

This new book takes Frankl's work to the next level by creating a framework on how to implement the work of Logotherapy, enriched by Rabbi Dovber's "*Tract on Contemplation*" and the "*Tract on Ecstasy.*" It provides the reader with a step-by-step guide on how to access the power of the soul via Logotherapy.

Ten Levels of Meaning

In order to structure Logotherapy and make it accessible to everyone including therapists and those who seek emotional wellness, I created the "*Ten Levels of Meaning*," which will help you explore your inner world, understand where you may be stuck and where to focus your attention right now. You will learn how to detect meaning on each level, starting from sensations in your body all the way up to the more elusive spiritual aspects of yourself.

CHAPTER 2:

The Psychology of the Spiritual Unconscious

**"The quest for meaning is the key to mental health
and human flourishing."**
Viktor E. Frankl, *Man's Search for Meaning*

I s there a place in psychology for meaning and spirituality? Standard therapy may not typically include connecting with your goodness, finding meaning, connecting with God, and actualizing spirituality. But what if these powerful resources *are* the road to psychologically overcoming depression, anxiety, or trauma?

In my experience, the cure for my clients' dilemmas is not found by directing them to focus on themselves, but by helping them to live with their values and actualizing their spiritual and creative potentials that lie deep within *and* beyond themselves.

Take Sarah, a forty-five-year-old woman who struggled with depression for over a decade. A previous marriage to an abusive husband led to a divorce, after which she remarried and developed a loving and stable relationship. Soon after her new marriage, she was diagnosed with Ankylosing Spondylitis, (AS), a debilitating autoimmune disease for which, the doctors informed her, there was no real cure. After her diagnosis, she struggled with a long bout of depression.

Despite the emotional and physical pain she was suffering, Sarah had a remarkably resilient and joyful personality. She was an inspiration to her friends and family members. Guided by Frankl's principle of focusing on values and spiritual strengths, I picked up on the theme of her resilience by asking her a seemingly simple question about her trauma. I didn't request that she merely recall what her trauma entailed, but about *how* she maintained such a powerful attitude despite it all.

Sarah responded, "Although previous therapy over the years hasn't fully helped me, I decided to work on my *emunah* (faith). I listen to classes day and night about trusting God. I also only surround myself with positive and optimistic people. At some point I decided to make a decision to focus on my future and not my past. I felt it was liberating."

Sarah, and others like her, demonstrate that traditional therapy has its limitations. She found that focusing on her beliefs and being optimistic worked better and helped her more than talking about herself. The key for her was not to delve further into her past wounds and traumas, but rather to focus her attention on her values and faith. As a result of redirecting her focus and attitudes toward spirituality, she was able to complete her journey toward long-lasting healing.

The *Religio* and Inner Goodness

According to Frankl, finding the unconscious drive towards spirituality and God is the key to profound emotional transformation. He viewed the unconscious as a reservoir filled with spiritual potential and referred to this unconscious Godly force as the *religio*, or "unconscious God."[1]

The term unconscious implies a built-in, innate orientation to God and meaning. And, unlike Freud who viewed the drives of the unconscious as being dark and destructive, Frankl's *religio* is constructive and drives a person toward meaning. It is this unconscious "core" that directs and orients a person's choices and actions to find and actualize values and spiritual purpose. It sits there waiting for you until you turn on the switch.

Solution-Focused Brief Therapy

As a therapist, I have always embraced the concept of my clients being authentically healthy in their core. It's like choosing where to shine the light. This positive orientation can change the outcome of therapy. Just ask yourself the question: How would you feel if a professional spent 50 minutes talking about what's wrong with you versus if he or she spoke about what's right about you?

The focus on positivity is influenced by my training in Solution-Focused Brief Therapy (SFBT). In SFBT the therapist focuses only on the positive parts of a person's experience. This moves the client from problem-saturated talk to solution-focused talk.[2] The focus on the positive creates a stark environmental change for both the therapist and client. Unlike traditional modalities, SFBT fosters a decidedly positive and optimistic environment by seeking out and relying on the client's natural resources. SFBT practitioners view clients as whole and resourceful. It maintains that clients have within them the resources and the solutions to their own problems.

Embracing Spirituality

According to Frankl, this holds true for spiritual yearnings as well. These spiritual sparks are positive emotional resources that need only be focused upon and highlighted. They tend to lie dormant unless we help the client focus on them and accept their influence. It is similar to finding coal under the rubble and blowing air over it to intensify its embers. Just a little bit of air brings the coal's heat to life and makes it burn bright.

In an interview about his book *The Unconscious God*, Frankl asserts that psychology needs to embrace man's inherent desire for spirituality, and when requested, to expand—and not minimize—his or her relationship with God:

Interviewer: I note that your latest book in English has an intriguing title, "The Unconscious God," and it occurs to me that this is an unusual title for a psychiatrist to give to one of his books. I wonder if you'd comment a bit on that book.

Frankl: It's a deplorable state of affairs that such a title should be unusual or challenging a psychiatrist because it depicts the actual situation, and this is that for too long a time psychiatry has closed its eyes toward a phenomenon such as a religion, because religion is also a human phenomenon. Any human phenomenon should have been taken into account and taken at face value by psychiatry.

Instead, for too long a time as I said before, psychiatry and more specifically psychoanalysis [Sigmund Freud], has tried to convince us that religion is no more than just a collective compulsive obsessive neurosis of mankind; that God is no more than just the projection of a father image and so forth. And what I think is that psychiatry, or for that matter psychology, should remain open without selecting certain phenomena that it allows to be existent; it should be open to all human phenomena.

One of the most important phenomena in human life is man's reaching out for a meaning to his existence and [especially] when he's reaching out for an *ultimate meaning*. Believing in the existence of ultimate meaning *is* the root or the crown of religion. And in the widest possible sense, religion is an entirely human phenomenon and has to be taken at its face value rather than being dismissed as a symptom of neurosis.[3]

Descending Lower, Reaching Higher

What distinguishes Logotherapy from Freudian psychoanalysis or "depth" psychology (going deep into one's childhood issues) is that Frankl maintains that the "lower" a person descends into the trials and tribulations of life, the "higher" he must reach to access more refined levels of consciousness. For example, when you descend into a deep pit you will need a long rope to pull you out from the bottom. But if you find yourself in a shallow ditch, you may easily climb out. Freud would suggest that you figure out how you got to the bottom of the pit in the first place; Frankl asks that we focus our attention upwards and reach higher to climb out.

Overestimating Greatness

Frankl compared emotional growth to a pilot overestimating his flight's destination. So too, a person needs to have a higher vision of what he *should* become.

If there's an airplane flying from the West to the East, from point A to point B, and there's a crosswind blowing from the North to the South, [then] if the pilot aims directly at Point B, he will drift South of his destination to point C. Instead, he must aim North of his destination to point D so that the crosswind will bring him where he intends to go. This is exactly what Goethe said: "If we take man as he is, we make him worse, but if we take man as he should be, we make him capable of becoming what he can be.

And now you will understand why one of my writings once said this is the most ab maxim motto for any psychotherapeutic activity. So if you don't recognize a young man's will to meaning, man's search for meaning, you make it worse: you make him dull, you make him frustrated, and you still add and contribute to his frustration. In this so-called criminal or juvenile or drug abuser and so forth there must be what we call a spark of search for meaning. So let's recognize this. Let's presuppose it, and then you will elicit it from him and you will make him become what he, in principle, is capable of becoming.[4]

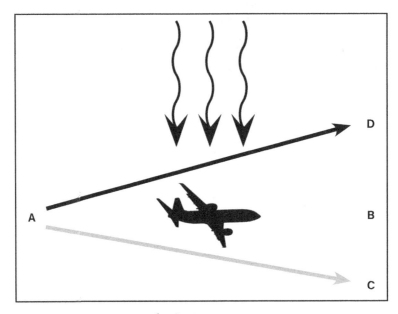

Moshe's Depression

Using Frankl's principle of "overestimation," let's take the case of Moshe, 33, as an example. Over the course of many years, he suffered from depression and marijuana addiction, and he had been on antidepressants since his teenage years. Despite engaging in therapy and taking medication, Moshe was still experiencing feelings of self-hatred and meaninglessness.

He was employed in a high-powered job that brought him fame and recognition. However, he shared with me that he was, "Stuck in a field where I do not agree with the political orientation of the company I'm working for. No matter what I do, I persistently feel that I do not share the same values with my directors. I always dreamed of helping people, but now I'm just a cog in a wheel, protecting my job to maintain my lifestyle. I'm feeling like my life is meaningless."

Since Moshe had already seen several therapists over the past decade,

I decided to take a different approach. As opposed to the cognitive behavioral work he had experienced with previous therapists, I decided to pull out a copy of *Man's Search for Meaning* and share with him what Frankl said:

> A man who becomes aware of his responsibility to a human being who affectionately waits for him, or to a work that remains unfinished, will never be able to throw away his life." By knowing "why" he exists, he can bear almost any "how."[5]

I then asked Moshe what areas in his life he would like to take more responsibility for. He told me he wanted to work with disadvantaged teenagers and felt that this would bring him a greater feeling of purpose in his life and more happiness.

Talking to Your Future Self

I also introduced Moshe to a Logodrama technique I call "Talking to Your Future Self." Here, a person visualizes his or her self in the later parts of their life and asks for advice as they reflect on the accomplishments and experiences that had made their life worth living.

After a few moments of contemplation, Moshe shared with me that he envisioned himself in his 80s looking back at a number of priorities in his life: to become a musician, to travel and experience different places and cultures in the world, to go into recovery, and to help children out of poverty.

I encouraged Moshe to listen to his future self and take a new direction in his life and follow his dreams. Eventually, he decided to quit his job, take up music lessons, and travel abroad with the savings he had accumulated over the years. He told me that when he returned, he joined a 12-step group for his addiction, and he started working in an inner-city program for disadvantaged and neglected youth. At our next meeting, he reported that he had never felt so happy in his life and that many of his symptoms of depression had disappeared.

I also shared with Moshe the living example of Rabbi Yitzi Hurwitz who suffers with the debilitating symptoms of Lou Gehrig's disease, ALS, which has rendered him immobile and paralyzed all parts of his body except his eyes. He is the father of seven children and the spiritual leader at Chabad Jewish Center in Temecula, California. Despite the disease he continues to galvanize others to find meaning in their lives.

In his article "Breaking through a Dark Place in Your Life," Rabbi Hurwitz writes:

> There are times in a person's life when everything is dark, either for you or someone you know. What can you do to help yourself in this situation, which my wife calls "the pit"? This is what I learned from my wife Dina. The pit is a useful place, because every time you are in the pit, you have to learn new coping skills in order to climb out. Sometimes it's going to be a small thing that is going to pull you out of your slump. . . .
>
> It takes a lot of light to break the darkness. Once you have a coping skill, it will remain with you and you will be able to tap into that when going gets tough.[6]

In order to turn his challenge into a triumph, Rabbi Hurwitz has to access higher spiritual and emotional resources. As Frankl writes in *Man's Search for Meaning*:

> We who lived in concentration camps can remember the men who walked through the huts comforting others, giving away their last piece of bread. They may have been few in number, but they offer sufficient proof that everything can be taken from a man but one thing: the last of the human freedoms—to choose

one's attitude in any given set of circumstances, to choose one's own way.

And there were always choices to make. Every day, every hour, offered the opportunity to make a decision, a decision which determined whether you would or would not submit to those powers which threatened to rob you of your very self, your inner freedom; which determined whether or not you would become the plaything of circumstance, renouncing freedom and dignity to become molded into the form of the typical inmate.[7]

In my experience as a psychotherapist, and as described by Rabbi Hurwitz, attitudes are often a more lucrative place to focus than childhood issues. Attitudes have more influence on an individual's emotional reality. The attitude that a person adopts—not the circumstances he is thrust into—often determines his ability to overcome even the most difficult emotional challenges.

Clients suffering from chronic depression, anxiety, or OCD can witness this in their therapy. Often, they have been suffering for years and turned to therapy to resolve their problems. Too often, they continue to find themselves having difficulty coping with their symptoms such as lethargy, low energy, panic attacks, and invasive and repetitive negative thoughts.

It is at this point that logotherapists ask clients to take a stand in the face of their overwhelming physical and emotional symptoms, to utilize their ability to self-detach, and to choose their attitudes. Even while all of a person's internal signals are pointing in the opposite direction, values of calmness, equanimity, and faith can help them maintain balance in their life.

Clients need to keep their focus on actualizing values and achieving goals. When they do so, they are more likely to overcome their challenges, and at a more rapid pace.

Meditative Moment. Think of a time where you faced an insurmountable challenge and you turned to a meaningful or spiritual resource (God, purpose, value) that helped you through that period of your life. If you are experiencing an emotional impediment in your life right now, introduce a higher spiritual value in the equation and see how it works out.

For reducing chronic depression or anxiety, an individual must be focused on accessing higher parts of their consciousness, or what we will refer to as "levels of meaning," in order to heal. If the client is not initially aware of these potentials, it is the therapist's job to help them uncover these sparks. My objective is to point out to them what they already know intuitively and to magnify their significance. I often view this process as a sailor catching a wind to lift up his sails in the right direction.

"I broke my neck, but it did not break me."

One of Viktor Frankl's students, Jerry Long, provided an example of man's inherent greatness and ability to transform life by living with his values and by changing his attitude. As a budding sportsman in 1978, Long dreamed of playing baseball. However, a tragic diving accident left him quadriplegic. As he lay paralyzed in his hospital bed he had to choose between despair and hopelessness or empowerment to fulfill a new purpose or meaning in his life.

Despite his condition, Long decided to help others who had experienced similar accidents or illnesses to overcome their pain by finding meaning in their lives. This led to his connection with Frankl, who invited him to speak at an international conference of Logotherapy, where he shared his perceptions of life in the face of dire circumstances similar to Frankl's at Auschwitz.

Frankl and Long shared a remarkable encounter about suffering and finding meaning:

Interviewer: Dr. Frankl you have written that there are three ways to find meaning, one being in adopting an attitude toward a fate which cannot be changed—and in Jerry's case it seems to me that's what Logotherapy has done for you. You have a permanent disability, a severe disability, and there's nothing much you can do about that, but what you do have control over is your attitude. Could you tell us how Logotherapy helped to shape your attitude?

Long: I think that it's important to remember my attitude-adoption and the Logotherapy that I employed initially was without any knowledge of Logotherapy. I had not read any books and I had no acquaintance with it but, intuitively, I modified my attitude toward the situation. In one particular line that Dr. Frankl quotes fairly often, "I broke my neck, it didn't break me." I had a physical constraint that I had to deal with, which I could not change. I had no ability to suddenly walk again. However, I did have the ability to choose to live and at least attempt a meaningful life in spite of that physical disability.

Interviewer: I think that substantiates your theory that within the human being is this innate searching for meaning, and it sounds like that's what you were doing, Jerry. And then when you read Dr. Frankl's work, it all fit together, and you realized that this was exactly how you had been thinking all along.

Long: When I read his book, I was overcome with a sense of deja vu because several times he spoke of reactions and the way he felt and the way he interpreted his experiences in the concentration camps. And repeatedly were the times when I identified personally: I felt the exact same way when I lay in that hospital bed as he did when he was in a concentration camp.

Frankl: It's also a compliment what Jerry says—a compliment for Logotherapy in a strange way inasmuch as usually, each one who comes up with the so-called new therapeutic or other scientific approach prides himself to offer something new. As he said right before, whereas we are proud to just dig out to make people more aware, more conscious of something that has been within themselves built-in, as it were, all along: the "wisdom of the heart" that is referred to in the Psalms.

In Logotherapy, what I am used to calling the pre-reflective ontological self-understanding, is just the fact that man knows all along intuitively, as he put it, what life is all about: that life is a chain of unique situations implying unique potentialities to be actualized in a meaningful way. So the possibilities to invest meaning in our lives, or for that matter each single life situation, are virtually infinite. Because, as you were hinting to right before, there are various ways or avenues leading up to true meaning fulfillment. And if one avenue is closed, then you have still others. And it's up to the intuition of a really alert spirit as that of Jerry's to find out if I can do that—he said physically or mentally or spiritually. If I cannot use this, I have to turn to another one. There are always possibilities and always alternatives and he made use of this fact on the grounds of his immense intuitive capacity. We are just verbalizing in Logotherapy the marvelous unconscious or, better to say, implicit wisdom of the man in the street. This is a compliment that makes us proud.

Interviewer: So it's calling the potential, but that is within.

Frankl: It is the awareness of the potentials in here as potentialities waiting to be actualized.

Interviewer: I think your quote in *Man's Search for Meaning* is that "we should not ask what we can expect from life but rather what life expects from us."

Frankl: Right; it is the Copernican switch turning the great, maybe the greatest question on the lips or in the hearts of any human being (albeit more often than not on an unconscious level) into the reverse. Actually, there is implied the fact that actually it's not up to us to ask the question *What is the meaning of life?* But upon closer scrutiny we might become aware, in the final analysis, that we are those who are asked: that life is asking questions to us, questions we can only answer not by verbal replies but by action. By doing something. Each situation confronting us implies a question. But this question can only be answered by our deeds, by our acting, by our behavior. And if need be, if the situation necessitates, just to shoulder it, because we cannot do anything about it: for instance, a more or less permanent handicap. In such a case what we can change is ourselves: changing the sense of rising above the situation and growing beyond ourselves."[8]

In 1998, Jerry Long commemorated the passing of Viktor Frankl. In it he wrote: "Once, after speaking to a large audience, I was asked if I ever felt sad because I could no longer walk. I replied, 'Professor Frankl can hardly see, I cannot walk at all, and many of you can hardly cope with life. What is crucial to remember is this: We don't need just our eyes, just our legs, or just our minds. All we need are the wings of our souls and together we can fly.'" [9]

Takeaways

- The unconscious mind is filled with remarkable meaningful and spiritual resources that can help restore emotional imbalance and overcome depression, anxiety, and PTSD.
- To reduce depression or anxiety a person may be better off to look for spiritual "height" as opposed to psychological "depth."
- The lower a person feels, the higher they need to reach.
- There are different possibilities that exist in the unconscious mind, potentially both good and bad. The good is a powerful resource for emotional growth.
- Values can help a person overcome depression, anxiety, and PTSD.

Questions for Self-Exploration

- Has psychology negatively influenced the view you have of yourself?
- Do you believe that your "essence" is not good? If so, where did that belief come from?
- Can you find an alternative way of looking at yourself from a spiritual perspective?
- How could finding the bright light within yourself influence your feeling of depression, anxiety, or PTSD?
- What are your ultimate values that you are willing to commit to in order to live a better life?

CHAPTER 3:

The Ten Levels of Meaning

"Man is originally characterized by his 'search for meaning' rather than his 'search for himself.' The more he forgets himself — giving himself to a cause or another person — the more human he is. And the more he is immersed and absorbed in something or someone other than himself the more he really becomes himself."
Viktor E. Frankl, *Man's Search for Meaning*

We have learned that connecting with your spirituality is a powerful way to achieve rapid emotional healing. In fact, many people are able to access these levels without even being aware of their existence, until now. The Ten Levels of Meaning can be visualized in the following diagram.

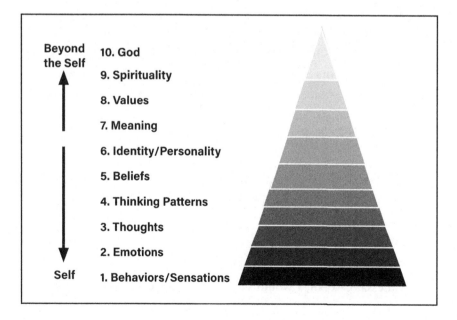

Each level represents an internal resource, such as a value or a meaningful activity, which can be utilized for transforming one's emotions as the following story describes. A few years ago, a woman named Vanessa Chesters, who lives in rural Western Canada, signed up for my online course in trauma at torahpsychology.org. Vanessa was no ordinary student. She is a 38-year-old mom of three children who broke her neck while diving in a pool in Florida. Her injury is known as a "hangman's fracture," which was made famous by Christopher Reeve after he fell from a horse and became paralyzed. In our conversation, she shared how she survived and what values she focused on to become more resilient for herself and her family.

While Vanessa's fracture never fully healed and she was still in pain, she survived because she decided to live with a value that helped her through the darkest days of her life. In our interview, I asked her what gave her the strength to overcome her near-death experience (the full dialogue can be found in chapter 9):

DS: Vanessa, when you were lying in the hospital bed just after your accident, what gave you courage to go on?

Vanessa: I had read Viktor Frankl's book *Man's Search for Meaning*. It was one of those books that impressed me . . . that in a dire situation, man's ability to get through those circumstances on the basis of perspective is quite significant.

DS: In what way?

Vanessa: It helped me realize that in those difficulties there's hope, and it really comes down to how you perceive the experience.

DS: And what else?

Vanessa: Overall, I would say, too, that what helped me most is that I chose to concentrate on what was working, and not on what wasn't working. So if I had some pain going on I choose to focus on the thought that I'm so lucky that I'm here for a second chance at life and I'm here to help my toddlers, you know, get up in the morning and give them breakfast.

DS: How were you able to do that?

Vanessa: I was unsure at that point what was going to be at that moment. It was a very scary moment. I mean I had my children in bed that night at home knowing they were there at the scene. . . . There were so many things that were going through my mind and I wasn't going to be there for them in the morning the next day. I was like "if they did see me in the next few days I would look significantly different." I had compression on my spine and then on my throat so I couldn't talk very well. And it was just this realization that that was a near-death experience. In my mind I was like, I can't believe that happened and at first there was a lot of blame that I went through in terms of like, "How could I have done that?" and "How did I not judge the possibility of death?"

DS: With all this running through your mind, what did you do to survive?

Vanessa: I guess it's that I also realized that I was still here for a reason; there was a purpose. Now, I wasn't calm, that's for sure, when I was in the hospital and all this happened. I wasn't calm because the processing of all those things at the same time almost caused reversion to a childlike state at first—that is, until I could break it into small pieces: you know, "How am I gonna get through this once I have the halo on?" and "What am I going to say to my kids?" and "How am I going to project resilience to them?" And I think "resilience" is the only word that I can think of in my mind that describes what I wanted to show them in my scenario.

DS: Where did the resilience come from? How did you evoke that?

Vanessa: Because the first time, and it's forever burnt into my mind, when my three-year-old came to see me in the hospital he was immediately in a fear-based state. You could see it all over his face. He sees his mother in a metal contraption, this halo, lying in a medical bed and trying to process what's happened. He didn't even really know what was going on—let's be real about that. And then my five-year-old just completely did not know what to say either.

And to help them feel comfortable at the time, the *Transformers* movie was such a big hit (this is a number of years ago) so I said to them, "Mom's doing okay now." I was in a lot of pain, but I didn't tell them that. "But guess what the cool thing is? You'll be able to show me at show-and-tell to your class. I'm gonna be like a "transformer." That's what this is. It's like a metal contraption, like in *Transformers*." And then their faces softened and they became more comfortable with the circumstance because I was trying to relate to something that would resonate with them and not thinking about how I was feeling. So putting myself in their shoes I would say that actually helped me to move forward because I wanted to show them that *no matter what we go through in life it's how we deal with it that makes the difference—what we choose to focus on versus what we don't focus on makes the difference—and we have that power in ourselves to do that.*[1]

It was Vanessa's choice to live by her values that allowed her to survive: to teach her children that no matter what challenges they may face, they have the power to choose how they react. Individuals like Vanessa, who have no formal training in psychotherapy, can offer us insight into how real people overcome seemingly hopeless situations.

The Ten Levels of Meaning

You've heard now from Viktor Frankl, Rabbi Yitzi Hurwitz, Jerry Long, and Vanessa Chesters. Each of them endured agonizing difficulties in their lives yet developed ways to rise above and hold on to a powerful sense of hope and optimism.

We will describe each level in detail and demonstrate how it can be applied to your everyday life. Pay attention, as these ten levels or steps are your key to gaining an understanding of your unique spiritual potentials, and how to utilize them for healing.

Level	Dimension	Questions	
1	Behaviors/ Body Sensations (Somatic)	How are you behaving? What are you sensing in your body?	Finite (limited)
2	Emotions / Feelings	What are you feeling?	
3	Thoughts	What are you thinking?	
4	Thinking Patterns/Traps	What are your habitual think-ing patterns?	SELF
5a	Beliefs about yourself	What do you believe about yourself?	
5b	Beliefs about others	What do you believe about others?	
6	Identity/ Personality	Who are you?	
7	Meaning	What is meaningful to you?	Beyond the Self
8	Values	What values are important to you?	
9	Spirituality / Purpose / Mission	What is your purpose?	
10	Spiritual Essence	What is your essence?	Infinite Unlimited

Finding Your Own Levels of Meaning

How can you explore your own levels of meaning? We begin with Level One, Behaviors/Sensations. The quickest way to understand yourself is by observing how you feel in your body. Close your eyes, take a deep breath, and ask yourself, "What do I feel in my body right now?" Perhaps you're feeling tension, pain, tingling, or a tightness in your chest? A specific emotional state is usually accompanied by some form of activation or sensation in the body. An aching stomach or racing heart may symbolize a person's fear or worry about an upcoming event.

Similarly, what are you doing? Are you in a state of fight-or-flight and running away or avoiding your feelings? Do you feel like you're surrounded by darkness and are spending time alone isolating yourself from your friends and family? Make a note of what you are sensing in your body and what you are doing right now.

Emotions

Next, follow your emotions (level 2). Are you feeling sad, scared, or angry? Remember that emotions come from the Latin *emovere*, which means "to move."A person's emotions convey what they are experiencing and move them to act. Are you feeling terribly sad or anxious right now? Perhaps you're feeling angry that you didn't get something you wanted or fearful you may not get something you want in the future? Make a note of your emotions.

Thoughts

Now, follow "upward" in the chart from your emotions to your thoughts (level 3). Remember that emotions do not exist in a vacuum. They emerge from underlying thoughts, which can be positive or negative in nature. If you are feeling anxious, you are probably having negative thoughts like: "I cannot cope," "This is too overwhelming," or "Nothing seems to be working out for me." If you are feeling good, it's likely your thoughts are positive and self-nurturing. Make a note of your thoughts.

The founder of Cognitive Behavioral Therapy (CBT), Dr. Aaron Beck, explained the connection between thoughts, feelings, and behaviors/sensations. He believed that consciousness progresses on different levels. In other words, thoughts create feelings, and feelings create behaviors and bodily sensations.[2] While treating his patients for depression or anxiety, he noticed that the vast majority reported negative thoughts that caused them to have negative emotions, which led to unhealthy behaviors or overwhelming somatic sensations (heart racing, rapid breathing, or even lethargy).

Thinking Patterns

Where do people's thoughts come from? According to Beck, they originate from thinking patterns (level 4), also known as cognitive distortions or "thinking traps." Here are some of the thinking traps that may resonate with you:

- Black-and-white thinking. Thinking of possible outcomes only at either extreme (good or bad) and not seeing all the possible outcomes in-between (or the "gray"). Most of life is somewhere in the middle.
- Overgeneralizing. Making sweeping judgments about ourselves (or others) based on only one or two experiences. These thoughts typically contain the words "always" and "never." The problem: you can never be summed up in one word or base your value as a person on only one single experience!
- Catastrophizing. This involves believing that everything will turn out negatively and that you're in a worse situation than you really are.

- Magnifying or minimizing. Exaggerating your mistakes or minimizing your successes or good points.
- Negative filtering. Focusing only on the negative without letting in the positive.
- Labeling. Thinking critically and using negative words to describe ourselves and others. This kind of thinking is unhelpful and unfair.
- "Should" Statements: This is when you tell yourself how you "should," "must," or "ought to" feel and behave. However, this is *not* how you actually feel or behave. The result is that you are constantly anxious and disappointed with yourself and/or with others around you.
- Personalizing. Believing that you are entirely to blame for something even though you had little or nothing to do with the outcome. In fact, the situation may not be connected to you in any way at all.
- Overestimating danger. This is when we believe that something that is unlikely to happen is actually right around the corner. It's not hard to see how this type of thinking can maintain your anxiety. For example, how can you not feel scared if you are constantly worrying that you may suddenly suffer a heart attack at any time? [3]

Let's take the thinking trap called "black and white thinking." In essence, it is an extreme way of thinking where people view themselves on either end of an extreme spectrum believing they are either good or bad, safe or unsafe, successful or a failure, attractive or ugly. There are no gray areas in between; it's either this way or that way. For example, if your thought is, "I am going to fail the test," it is probably influenced by the extreme way in which you view yourself. It is black and white thinking. There is no room in your mind for thinking, "I may get a B or even a C+ on the test, but that doesn't mean I will fail."

Meditative Moment. What are your thinking traps? How do they distort the way you view your life? What would your life look like without these thinking traps?

Beliefs

What causes us to fall into thinking traps like "black-and-white thinking"? The answer to this question is that your thinking traps emerge from the beliefs you maintain about yourself and others (Levels 5a and 5b).

For example, say you're lying in bed under the covers at midnight drifting off to sleep, and you hear a rattling noise by the window. If you believe that the noise is the sound of a robber breaking into the house, you feel fear. You may begin to have a panic attack and your heart starts racing and you scream or call the police.

The same holds true when you maintain the opposite belief. If you believe the rattling at the window is only leaves blowing in the wind, you will feel calmer and go back to sleep. Your belief that there was no danger allowed you to think more clearly and feel more relaxed. According to the diagram below, this results in a very different outcome in your behavior.

Beliefs are the emotional GPS that guide us on how we think and feel. The negative beliefs we maintain about ourselves and others, especially the ones connected to depression or anxiety, revolve around three core concepts: worthlessness, helplessness, or feeling unlovable. Many of these beliefs are formed as a result of trauma or difficult circumstances—such as childhood abuse, invalidating or emotionally ill parents, accidents, war, or persistent emotional stress.

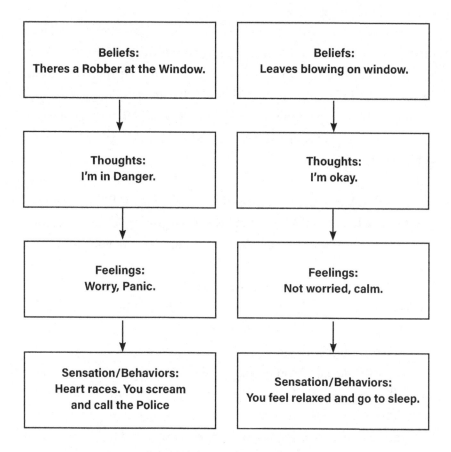

Beliefs: Theres a Robber at the Window.	Beliefs: Leaves blowing on window.
Thoughts: I'm in Danger.	Thoughts: I'm okay.
Feelings: Worry, Panic.	Feelings: Not worried, calm.
Sensation/Behaviors: Heart races. You scream and call the Police	Sensation/Behaviors: You feel relaxed and go to sleep.

David's Obsession

Take the case of David, a 45-year-old businessman who came to my office for help with depression. David's neighbor erected a new fence between their properties and painted it black. Since then, David reported feeling depressed, irritated and consumed with fighting his neighbor.

As David obsessed about how the color had ruined the aesthetics of his backyard, he began to doubt the value of his home, which he considered to be the culmination of his life's work. Adding insult to injury, he believed his neighbor painted the fence black on purpose to upset him. The night before David came to see me, his anger at his neighbor became so overwhelming that he was unable to fall asleep.

From a purely factual point of view, it is difficult to understand how the color of a fence could cause depression. However, according to our levels of meaning we can understand why David felt those emotions. A lack of self-esteem, an internal belief that he was "worthless," and distorted thinking patterns drove David's emotions. His feelings of anger, resentment, and frustration were rooted not in the fence, but in his childhood experiences.

Meditative Moment. What negative beliefs do you hold on to that influence how you feel and behave? What preferred beliefs could you adopt about yourself that would improve your life?

Where do our beliefs come from? Our beliefs are formed by our personality/identity (level 6) which is a product of how we are raised, our family's culture, values (or lack thereof), and economics, as well as their relationship with God.

When exploring David's family, he shared with me that he came from a family that was critical, invalidating, and at times abusive. Growing up he felt he was not worthy of love or kindness from others. He developed a personality style that was reactive and defensive, and he often got into interpersonal conflicts with people in his life.

Indeed, our personalities are formed by factors we cannot control. Yet, in order to help ourselves ascend to the next level of thinking (levels seven and above), we need to reach beyond ourselves and transcend our emotional inheritance.

Choosing Levels of Thinking Beyond Yourself

Both Jerry Long and Vanessa Chesters were able to reach higher and think on different levels *beyond* themselves. Instead of seeing themselves as victims, they chose to see themselves as survivors. Their new ways of thinking went beyond identity, beliefs, thought patterns, thoughts, feelings, and sensations. Instead, they shifted their thinking towards meaning, values, and spirituality (levels 7 and above).

Finding Meaning in Auschwitz

This was the same shift Frankl made in the concentration camps that he spoke about in *Man's Search for Meaning*. After serving as a psychiatrist in Vienna for many years, he was deported to Auschwitz in 1942, where both of his parents and his wife were murdered. He endured suffering in multiple concentration camps. He faced abuse, torture, and starvation. Despite his suffering, he described how his experiences in the camps reaffirmed his convictions and theories that he had formed earlier in life.

Remarkably, long before the war started, Frankl had developed the principles of Logotherapy. His manuscript was already written when the Nazis stole it from him at the gates of Auschwitz, and he faced the possibility that he or his work, or both, might not survive. In utter despair, he asked himself: Does the publication of my book determine the meaning of my life? In Auschwitz, he chose to focus on alternative meanings he could uncover, despite facing inescapable suffering.

His first concern was to survive for his family, or to help other inmates in Auschwitz who were in despair.[4] Next, he turned to helping others in the camp to change their attitude towards their suffering. According to survivors of Auschwitz who knew him well, Frankl organized weekly discussion groups on mental health and prompted other inmates to reflect on their past achievements. He encouraged them to contemplate on what values and meanings they would actualize after they were liberated from the camps.

Frankl even used this technique to survive on a death march. He imagined himself teaching his class as a way of finding meaning and hope in the midst of the Nazi concentration camps. He believed that by envisioning a future goal, he could endure the present suffering and survive the ordeal. Frankl understood that even when everything is stripped away from a person, they can still choose their attitude and their values. And in the same way, a therapist needs to help their clients choose their attitude in the sea of their depression or anxiety. From a psychological perspective, changes may be subtle, but they are profound. It may occur when a person resists the temptation to be overwhelmed by small inconveniences, when he or she confronts larger challenges in life, or when one chooses a spiritual path.

Menu of Meaning and Values

Meaning and values are unlimited concepts you can choose from. Every moment of life provides an opportunity to find meaning in the moment by infusing it with your values (levels 7 and 8). It all depends on *how* you interpret those moments, and *how* you react. What may be perceived as a challenge by some may be seen as an opportunity by others.

Here is one of the ways I've incorporated this in therapy. When one of my clients report feeling depressed or anxious, I ask them to choose some values that are important to them such as:

- Altruism
- Calmness
- Commitment
- Courtesy
- Fairness
- Family
- Faith
- Fidelity
- Gratitude
- Generosity
- Honesty
- Integrity

- Joy
- Kindness
- Maintaining healthy boundaries
- Morality
- Patience
- Positivity
- Reliability
- Self-control
- Selflessness
- Sensitivity

I then ask them to commit to three specific ways (meaningful actions) they can actualize these values in between our weekly meetings. For example, if they choose kindness, I ask them to think of three ways that they can be kinder at work or with their friends and family. If they choose generosity, I challenge them to commit to three generous acts to fulfill every week.

I often look upon this as sending somebody off on a treasure hunt where the client spends the week focused on experiencing meaning and looking for it in different areas of their life. After doing so, the vast majority report feeling less depressed or anxious. This occurs because experiencing meaning helps them de-reflect from the "self" by seeking ways of living a more meaningful life.

Meditative Moment. What are your top three values? How would living with your values change your life? Take one example of something that annoys you and then call upon a value like love, objectivity, or morality, and see what results ensue.

Identifying your values is one thing but you also need a way to *actualize* them. According to William Ryan, a professor of psychology who writes extensively on Logotherapy, "a value is something worthwhile that a person or persons could choose; a meaning is the value that a person or persons actually do choose." As he explains:

> Values take no initiative. It is existence which takes initiative by actually choosing values. Values are as passive as books on the shelves of a library; the larger the library, the wider the selections, like the Library of Congress. Of themselves, books contain no knowledge. They are bound sheets of paper that take up space. Meanings are like the actual choices that people make to take down the books and read them and learn from them. Prior to choosing, the value has no effect whatsoever upon the actual life of existence. One may call these values "noble" and "uplifting," but only inasmuch as one witnesses such values when they are transformed by free choice into meanings embodied in the concrete actions of a person throughout their lives. Only then, strictly speaking, does the value become a meaning.[5]

Creative, Experiential, and Attitudinal Values

Frankl spoke of the importance of finding meaning by actualizing three core values—including creative, experiential and attitudinal values. By doing so, one creates meaningful experiences and interactions.[6]

Creative values are actualized when a person uses his mind to create new realities. For example, when a teacher teaches, a doctor heals, and a therapist helps a client improve their emotional well-being, they find meaning through their work and in what they create.

Experiential values emerge when a person experiences someone or something outside of themselves. The most basic form of experiencing someone is through loving them via acts of kindness, even when you don't expect anything in return. Love, in this sense, means giving to the person for the very sake of giving. It also means experiencing the true essence of the other individual as a unique person deserving of love.

Another way you can experience meaning is by *encountering* something. This may take the form of listening to music, exercise, reading, painting, and other forms of artistic expression. It may also include going into nature and experiencing the wonders of the world through hiking, climbing, or simply gazing up at the stars and being in wonder about the creation of vast star systems and the universe.

Overcoming Trauma

Attitudinal values are attitudes we choose when faced with inescapable situations as witnessed by the stories of Jerry Long, Viktor Frankl, and Vanessa. Frankl describes this as "squeezing out" meaning in difficult situations. Examples would include a mother who experienced a still-birth, who uses it as an opportunity to help other women facing the same tragedies in their lives; a Holocaust survivor who lectures about man's inhumanity to man; a child of parents who were divorced who becomes a marriage therapist.

During a Logotherapy session, clients are encouraged to explore these three types of values and to work to effectuate and integrate them into their lives. And while doing so, I have found that many of my clients desire to go one step further and explore the source of their values (Levels 9 and 10), which we will discuss in the following chapter.

Takeaways

- A person's sense of self is built upon several levels of thinking, including bodily sensations, feelings, thoughts, beliefs, and their identity.
- Our beliefs affect how we perceive our reality and relate to others.
- To change feelings of depression or anxiety we need to change our beliefs.

Questions for Self-Exploration

- What are your perceptions of your surroundings and your relationships?
- Do you view life from a positive or negative perspective?
- Do you have negative beliefs that you can change that stymie or impede your life and keep you from being successful?
- Are your negative beliefs stemming from situations that happened to you or from thoughts and beliefs you have chosen?

CHAPTER 4:

What Happens When You Think about Meaning and God in Therapy

"Religion is the search for ultimate meaning."
—Viktor E. Frankl, *Man's Search for Meaning*

Connecting with one's spirituality has always been a way to feel uplifted and a means to find meaning in life. Since my childhood, I have been interested in the lives of those who overcame what would seem to be insurmountable challenges yet were able to pick themselves up and live life from a higher perspective. I was inspired by stories of people like Viktor Frankl, who, despite their trauma, were able to turn their tragedy into a triumph.

As a psychologist I am interested in understanding what happens to a person psychologically when they live with their spiritual values and start thinking about their relationship with God.

What I have witnessed is that those who live at the ninth and tenth levels of meaning perceive an interconnected pattern of life that weaves all reality together in a larger whole. They come in contact with a universal, creative force or Being, which allows them to answer the question *for whom* and not just *for what* is the purpose of their life.

Those who access their spirituality begin to see life from a broader perspective. They view themselves as being on a mission to fulfill their vision whether that vision is to cure hunger, heal sickness, bring world peace, or to increase the perception of Godliness in the world. While seeking the fulfillment of their spiritual perceptions they also experience greater feelings of happiness and joy.

Finding a Cause

If you are struggling with depression or anxiety, try finding a cause greater than yourself and see what happens. Consider someone who is feeling depressed, yet they commit, despite their symptoms, they go on a mission to feed the hungry or end poverty. The person looks to make a difference volunteering in their community and forms an organization to tell others about ways to get involved in the cause. This person travels from community to community hearing stories about poverty and violence and gathers resources to make a difference. No matter what happens they feel that life has a purpose, as they are in tune with a higher vision of themself.

Individuals on a mission don't get easily distracted by apathy or roadblocks. They rise above apathy and division by seeing oneness. They live their lives guided by the spiritual precept, "Love your neighbor as you love yourself." And they utilize every moment to fulfill their mission and purpose. There is little time to focus on their needs, as they are fully absorbed in making a difference in the world.

Meditative Moment. Have you ever been fully engrossed in a topic where you lost touch with time? What activities make you fully absorbed? Try doing one and see what happens.

Overcoming a Stillbirth

Living on the ninth level of meaning can change even the darkest moments in a person's life. Take Rivkah, age 40, who had recently lost her child in birth and was suffering from extensive trauma and Postpartum Depression (PPD). She had suffered from significant abuse as a child and believed that she didn't have a "voice" in the world. During our sessions, Rivkah explained to me that when a person has a stillbirth, they carry a significant amount of shame. Worse, a complete mourning experience does not occur as it does with the death of a loved one with a formed identity. Remember that the child's personality was never formed, yet a mother still has a deep emotional bond with the baby—a bond that most people could never understand.

Also, according to Rivkah, she felt that she never was allowed to have a "voice" to express her feelings, which is what she had also experienced as a child when she was abused by her parents. Rivkah had already gone through extensive psychotherapy, but she was still terribly depressed and agitated.

As a therapist guided by Logotherapy, I decided to try to help her to express her voice. Instead of digging deeper into her trauma, I asked her *what* she would like to accomplish in her life. She explained that she had always wanted to become a life coach and help others overcome their pain and suffering. By helping others find their "unheard" voice, she would find her own. I recommended a coaching program, which she then completed. After several months of training, she launched her own podcast and was working with several clients who had experienced personal loss.

A few months later Rivkah reported to me that she was feeling less despair and depression, and that she felt her life was getting "back on track." By connecting to her "higher" will and finding a new purpose, Rivkah was tapping into the most powerful psychological forces on the ninth level.

Rivkah's changes occurred through initially focusing on her trauma, but then the changes became more substantial by her pivoting to fulfill meaning in her life. When someone like Rivkah reaches higher, she becomes attuned to a life force feeling a greater sense of purpose with God. And, as she discovered, as you harness this energy you become a conduit for healing and an agent of change. You are no longer disappointed in yourself or your life, because you sense your purpose. You understand that the universe is not operating against but resonating through you.

From the ninth level, everything begins to make more sense. Your fight with your neighbor, your battles with feelings of inadequacy, and your frustrations with the lack of progress in your life are suddenly forgotten. This new sense of meaning has the power to ultimately heal your suffering.

We could not return her baby back to life, but we could give Rivkah a life of meaning to live for. This, in fact, has always been a custom in Judaism. For example, after the death of a loved one, family members and friends donate money to a cause. Some even choose to build an institution or form an entire organization around the memory of a loved one who has passed away.

Just think about the countless hospital wings, houses of worship, and research institutes that have been founded or funded "in memory of" someone who was lost. Jewish customs have always been sensitive to the need to find meaning in spite of one's loss. Logotherapy merely pointed this out from a psychological perspective.

Meditative Moment. Is there a trauma you could overcome by finding a purpose you could fulfill? What would that purpose or activity be? Helping others who are ill or poor? What cause can you donate to and attend their organization meetings?

Despair Is Suffering Minus Meaning (D=S-M)

When you find a meaning or purpose in your suffering you can avoid experiencing despair. Frankl described this phenomenon in an equation: "D=S-M" where despair (D) is suffering (S) minus meaning (M).[1] This implies that when one can find some meaning in their suffering, they will avoid falling into a state of despair, as he explained in *Man's Search for Meaning*:

> "Once, an elderly general practitioner consulted me because of his severe depression. He could not overcome the loss of his wife who had died two years before and whom he had loved above all else. Now, how can I help him? What should I tell him? Well, I refrained from telling him anything but instead confronted him with the question, "What would have happened, Doctor, if you had died first, and your wife would have had to survive you?" "Oh," he said, "for her this would have been terrible; how she would have suffered!" Whereupon I replied, "You see, Doctor, such suffering has been spared her, and it was you who have spared her this suffering—to be sure, at the price that now you have to survive and mourn her." He said no word but shook my hand and calmly left my office. In some way, suffering ceases to be suffering at the moment it finds a meaning, such as the meaning of a sacrifice."[2]

Frankl was able to show how even suffering may give a person the opportunity to become aware of a higher reality unknown before the trauma. With this knowledge, you can turn a "tragedy into a triumph" through realizing what purpose you live for. Not only is despair avoidable, but it may also turn out that it itself becomes an opportunity to experience a greater awareness of one's spiritual existence.

Meditative Moment. Consider exploring a possible meaning for some experience that has been difficult for you. How would finding meaning in your suffering change your life

This is not a simple emotional correction. It represents the revivification of one's life. It is a kind of rebirth where your soul is allowed to find peace in the universe, and you are free to fully actualize your inherent spiritual powers of creativity, curiosity, and optimism. With meaning, even trauma can be transformed into a tremendous source of energy that can change the world for good.

Overcoming Despair

Vanessa described this phenomenon when she explained how she attempted to avoid falling into a sense of despair before finding meaning, even in the face of breaking her neck:

"So my belief is if it didn't break me, it was a gift. The experience was a gift. It was a gift in that it helped me to enrich my life and now helps me help others get through something difficult by changing their mindset. During the recovery I was wearing a halo around my head and neck. No one could touch me at all. Before the accident I took things for granted like hugging my children. But I couldn't actually hug them and have that touch and that connection. It was one of the first things I was gonna do as soon as that halo came off because I didn't realize how I took for granted some basic things that we all think we have. I mean you interact with your family every day. You hug and you say I love you, but then that physical interaction when you don't have it is something that you just long for. And so when the halo came off or they told me it was coming off I was feeling this intense feeling of almost like *I can't wait for this freedom that I'm going to have, and what am I going to do with that freedom*, and then also the fear that was coming into my brain too, like *What does this mean for me now that the halo is coming off?* Well leading up to the halo coming off the conversation with my doctor was amazing— such a great physician. He had told me that the break was worse off than pre-halo so instead of it healing as it should have, I actually had displaced way more and he said, "But we're still taking the halo off today." I was like how could I have spent days in this halo that felt like jail and there was nothing physically that healed me? But then when it came off… that was some intense emotion right there. I was crying and—I just can't explain at all because it's just a moment where you're feeling freedom and fear at the same time.

DS: What else did you feel?

Vanessa: I felt gratitude, and the first thing that I did right after was hugged my kids and it was just such a wonderful feeling of appreciation and gratitude for getting a second chance at life.

DS: So, did you begin to see things differently?

Vanessa: Yes. It's an event that has impacted most things and for me specifically. I didn't see it as a bad thing, I saw it as a good thing, in fact, because it helped me be more aware of the power that goes along with perspective. And then also in that reflection, of the times when I might have thought I was a victim in a circumstance, when all in all, reality wasn't that bad.

Putting It All together

Returning to David's case (who suffered from depression that he ascribed to his neighbor painting his fence black), let's see how the power of Logotherapy and thinking on the ninth level can transform his life and help him respond differently. When confronted by the question of what to do about his neighbor, he needs to ask himself a question, "What is the purpose of my life?"

His answer may be: "The meaning of my life is to become a human being who overcomes petty emotions and circumstances by accessing a higher version of myself that reflects spiritual ideals and values such as patience, calmness and courage." Or, "The fence is an opportunity for me to fulfill a greater spiritual purpose. Just having my home exactly how I expect it to be is a function of my egocentric lifestyle. I prefer to see myself as representative of the greater good in the world, a representative of God, Who is focused on the needs of others."

Living on this new level of meaning can change everything. And, as you adopt a new attitude, you also change your thinking, feelings, and behaviors. What once seemed like an ominous impediment becomes a minor, passing inconvenience. The more light one shines, the greater chance you have to live on a higher emotional reality.

The Tenth Level and the Unconscious God

For some, however, just finding their spiritual purpose may not be sufficient to lift them from their state of depression or reduce their anxiety. They may find themselves in a situation, such as being in Auschwitz or facing inescapable suffering such as ALS, where they have to connect to their absolute core. They will need to contemplate on the highest level of meaning to be *with* God.

This tenth level is referred to in a Kabbalistic language as *Yechida* or total connection to God. In the Zohar, Rabbi Shimon Bar Yochai referred to this when he states, "Throughout the days of my connection to this world, I was bound to the Holy One—Blessed Be He—with a single knot...at one with Him."

The tenth level of meaning is reached by contemplating that everything is connected to God or, to use Kabbalistic language, that everything *is* God and there is nothing separate from Him. I am aware of the profundity of this statement. It is not easily digested in the Western world where rationalism and anti-dogmatic secular philosophy has equated being in rapture in God's presence, as being irrational, or worse, leading towards religious fundamentalism. This is not a Jewish concept. In Judaism, the more one senses oneself living inside God's reality, the calmer, more loving, and more connected a person feels and behaves.

The Kabbalists called this level of perception *soveiv* which means to be "encompassed." On a psychological level this can be experienced in the following guided meditation:

> Imagine yourself as a chip of stone thrown into water. See yourself floating down in a spiral form to the bottom of the lake. And as you settle down to the bottom of the lake, notice how you are feeling surrounded and safe. You forget yourself as you feel totally one with your environment as if you are a part of a wonderful system where everything exists together peacefully.

Now extend this metaphor to being "inside" of God where everything is seen as being fully encompassed by God's existence. However, this revelation is present in everything but not according to its level, since "All are equal before Him. As it is written (Yirmiyahu 23:24), 'For the heavens and the earth I fill.' I Myself—Hashem's Being and Essence, 'fills' the heavens and earth entirely equally."[3]

From this level of awareness emerges a greater sense of grounding and calmness, not irrational fundamentalism. Everything is connected, including all your inner parts and the world around you. Nothing is bad and nothing can harm you since it all comes from an infinite God who loves, protects, and guides you at all times. If used wisely, the tenth level of meaning can become a powerful source of self-regulation, calmness, and serenity.

Meditative Moment. Have you ever felt very close to God, as though He was intimately involved in your life guiding you? How do you feel when you go to the source of existence, beyond time and space, and fully connect to the Creator?

The Religio

The awareness that everything is one is the source of the *religio* noted by Frankl as the unconscious God. You may not be consciously aware of this, but it can be awakened at any time. For example, when you are having a bad day, but you decide to take a walk in the park and suddenly look up at the sky and perceive that everything is interconnected and makes sense. Or when you are faced with an inescapable situation and turn to God, knowing that only He can rescue you from your predicament. It can also be aroused when you face persecution and sacrifice your life for your values as witnessed throughout Jewish history.

Saying the Shema in Auschwitz

In *Man's Search for Meaning*, Viktor Frankl describes this experience of living on the tenth level of meaning and finding God, even in Auschwitz:

I had to undergo and overcome the loss of my mental child. And now it seemed as if nothing and no one would survive me; neither a physical nor a mental child of my own. So I found myself confronted with the question whether under such circumstances my life was ultimately void of meaning.

An answer to this question with which I was wrestling so passionately was already in store for me. . . . This was the case when I had to surrender my clothes and, in turn, inherited the worn-out rags of an inmate who had already been sent to the gas chamber. . . . Instead of the many pages of my manuscript, I found in a pocket of the newly acquired coat one single page torn out of a Hebrew prayer book, containing the most important Jewish prayer, *Shema Yisrael.* How should I have interpreted such a 'coincidence' other than as a challenge to *live* my thoughts instead of merely putting them on paper?[4]

What Viktor Frankl was referring to is that during the darkest hours of his life, he would turn to his source and utilize the power of *Shema,'* which translates to "Hear, O Israel, the Lord our God, the Lord is One." He was able to "hear" what exists deep within and to enter into the tenth level of thinking that even the Nazis could not separate him from. Yes, they could take away his food, his loved ones, his safety, and his shelter. They could beat and torture him, but they could not rob him of his highest value of being connected to God and living to sanctify His name.

Meditative Moment. Is there a trauma in your life that you can heal by going beyond yourself and connecting to God? How would enhancing that connection improve your life and emotions?

The *Tanya* refers to this essential connection while describing the process of the Creation of man in the Garden of Eden:

"And He breathed into his nostrils the breath of life," and "Thou didst breathe it [the soul] into me." And it is written in the *Zohar,* "He who exhales, exhales from within him," that is to say, from his inwardness and his innermost, for it is something of his internal and innermost vitality that man emits through exhaling with force.[5]

Thinking about your "Godly" self allows you to become aware that you are not merely your thoughts, feelings, or actions. Rather, that you have a soul that is beyond these three dimensions. The soul is given to you by God and is untainted by anything you do or feel. It is not affected by your parents, upbringing, or any traumas you may have suffered. It remains unblemished despite your mistakes or transgressions, as we read in the morning prayers "Lord, the soul that you have placed inside of me is pure. You created it, You formed it, You blew it into me. You protect it inside me. . . ." (*Siddur*, morning prayers).

Accordingly, this soul force is a force deep within us. It is experienced through every breath as though God Himself is breathing into us. And it is something that we may detect in the darkest moments of our lives.

Sudden Revelation of the *Religio*

Frankl maintained that the *religio* can spontaneously emerge even in the darkest moments. One of his clients who was hospitalized described how he suddenly experienced the tenth level of meaning:

When he was in a mental hospital where he felt like he was locked up as an animal in a cage and that no one came when he called to be taken to the bathroom... He was given daily shock treatment, insulin shock treatment, and sufficient drugs that he lost his awareness of life over the next few weeks.

However, in the darkness he acquired a sense of a higher connection. As he writes, "In the mental hospital, I acquired a sense of my own unique mission in the world. I knew then, as I know now, that I must have been preserved for some reason—however small, it is something that only I can do, it is vitally important that I do it. And because in the darkest moment of my life, when I was abandoned as an animal in a cage, when because of the forgetfulness induced by EST (Electric Shock Therapy) I could not call out to Him, He was there. In the solitary darkness of the 'pit' where men had abandoned me,

He was there. When I did not know his name, he was there, God was there."[6]

Another client of Frankl also experienced this new awareness in prison:

When a court psychiatrist came to visit me, I took an immense liking, right from the start, as he introduced himself with a very pleasant smile and a handshake, like I would still be somebody or at least a human being. Something deep and unexplainable happened to me from there on. I found myself living my life. That night, in the stillness of my small cell, I experienced a most unusual religious feeling which I never had before; I was able to pray, and with utmost sincerity, I accepted a higher will to which I have surrendered the pain and sorrow as meaningful and ultimate, not needing explanation.

From here on I've undergone a tremendous recovery. At the age of 54 I am at complete peace with myself and the world. I have found the true meaning of my life and time can only delay its fulfillment, but not deter it. I have decided to reconstruct my life and to finish my schooling. I am sure I can accomplish my goal. I have also found a new great source of unexpected vitality—I am now able to laugh over my own miseries, instead of wallowing in the pain of irrevocable failure.[7]

Frankl's client in prison experienced something "unexplainable." He speaks of an "unusual religious feeling," and through that he was able to accept a "higher will." He acquired a sense of a "higher connection" and thereby brought into consciousness his unique mission that he was "preserved" for.

Meditative Moment. Did you ever experience something unexplainable which made you feel connected to a higher will? What is the mission you are uniquely suited to fulfill?

Despite not knowing exactly what that mission was, whether it was miniscule or earth shattering, the simple act of consciously knowing it to be so, saved him. I believe that if this client had expressed those feelings to a Freudian-trained therapist, he would have analyzed this as a fantasy—a playing-out of his unconscious need to fulfill his Oedipal desire. In Logotherapy we view this as a revelation of the deepest expression of the *religio*.

Meditative Moment. Have you ever experienced an unconscious or Godly desire that could transform your life? Was this desire repressed, or did you try to actualize it? What latent desire could you act upon now?

Dream Analysis According to Frankl

One of the other unexpected places that we can detect the *religio* is through the analysis of dreams. Freud explored the idea that dreams offered the royal road to the unconscious mind. Frankl did not disagree with the importance of dream analysis. He recognized that Freud had indeed been able to develop techniques that were valuable in helping a person discover his unconscious motives. Frankl, however, questioned Freud's conclusions—and by extension, psychoanalytic conclusions. He challenged Freud's idea that symbols of man's desire for pleasure were hidden in the unconscious, and he rather assumed that it was driven by man's search for meaning.

In a fascinating recollection of a session with Frankl, a client reported a recurring dream where he found himself in another city and wanted to phone a family member. However, the dial on the phone was so large, it had over 100 numbers, and he never succeeded in placing the call. After waking up, he realized that the number he meant to dial was not his loved one, but that of a record company that was very successful financially.

It turned out that this client was a composer working for a company creating popular music that he did not enjoy. And, through the discussion of his dreams, he recounted spending a very satisfying time in a city and loved composing religious music. His professionally commissioned music did not bring him personal fulfillment. Upon interpretation, Frankl believed that the large dial signified the troubles he was having while making the choice about whether to stay with his company. In the German language, the word for dial is *Wählen* and the word for choice is *Auswahl*. Basically, these two words are interchangeable in that they share the same meaning. Frankl interpreted that the dial in the unhappy man's dream symbolized the choice he was facing.[8]

According to Frankl, the dream did not have anything to do with dialing a number; rather, it represented the conflict in the profession he chose: specifically, the choice between staying in a high paying job as an unsatisfied composer or becoming a writer of spiritual and religious music. The meaning of the dream became clear. He had been struggling to reconnect with his more spiritual side. And the choice looming in front of him, one he would eventually have to make, was greatly concerning him. According to Frankl, he was being driven by his *religio*, expressed as his desire to find his way back to a religious, artistic and meaningful vocation.

Meditative Moment: Looking back at your dreams, what religious symbols do you believe existed within them? What is your spiritual unconscious telling you? When you contemplate these thoughts, what do you feel in your body?

Putting It All Together

Focusing on your highest spiritual desires can be a powerful and transformative experience. From this perspective, tenth-level thinking cascades downwards, transforming all lower levels of thinking as we will see in the following diagram:

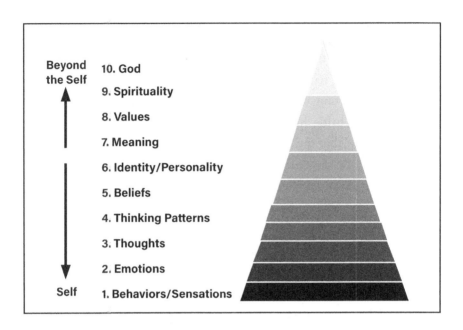

If one follows the chart from level ten downwards, you can see the powerful and cascading effect on all subsequent levels. When you contemplate, even briefly, on the belief that you are part of God and are taken care of by Him, you believe that there is a reason for everything that happens to you.

Every aspect of your life is therefore infused with a spiritual purpose that only you can uniquely fulfill (level 9). You maintain that in spite of your environment, you subscribe to values like patience (level 8) that are more important than instantaneous gratification. Not responding to difficult people or negative emotions become meaningful endeavors (level 7).

You then decide to choose your attitude and become a person of discernment and benevolence (level 6). Due to your attitude, you believe you are ultimately good (level 5a) and that others have inherent worth (level 5b). You become more optimistic (level 4) believing that you can deal with your life and your internal messages become positive (level 3). You then feel a pleasant sense of calmness and serenity (level 2), and then act with kindness towards your neighbor (level 1).

Yitzi Hurwitz and the Tenth Level of Meaning

Rabbi Yitzi Hurwitz is the greatest example of someone living life on the tenth level of meaning. Remember that, due to the debilitating effects of ALS, he can no longer speak but has to rely upon a computer to be his interpreter. In a powerful interview, Rabbi Yitzi spoke of a time when he couldn't use his eyes to type, stealing from him the one way by which he was communicating with the outside world:

> Over the past few weeks, I couldn't get my eyes to focus on the letters I wanted to write. Writing one word took as long as five minutes. I can't even begin to tell you how frustrating it was. I felt useless as a husband and father, not being able to write Torah articles. I felt irrelevant. I was in jail. What possible purpose could I have if I couldn't communicate? Brave and wise, Dina said to me, "On Shabbat when you don't use the eye gaze computer, you are still significant and relevant. Even if you can only see and look at people, that is meaningful to us. If you are alive, it means that you are relevant to Hashem and that you make a difference."
>
> What keeps me going is the realization that God is real, that He has a plan for the world, and that I am part of it. When you see it this way, instead of feeling down, when you are in a challenging situation you are filled with a sense of purpose, and you are lifted up. Your faith is tested. As well, I imagine I'm always talking to God: Sometimes it's "I'm exasperated. What do You want from me?" And sometimes it's "Wow, this is an amazing life that we get to live." And He encourages people to do good and be good all over the world. But I imagine perhaps His message is even more spiritual and has had greater impact absolutely. And messages of hope—to keep going, that God is with you and your struggles— have strengthened both of our faith. He's really my entire world, and as long as He's in it my world is a good place.[9]

From the perspective of the tenth level, Rabbi Yitzi envisioned himself as a "part of God from above," which cascaded downwards into the ninth level of his spiritual power of being a representative of God's goodness in the world. He finds ultimate meaning by viewing his predicament as an opportunity to actualize his potential spiritual powers (level 9). As he states in the same video:

> Hashem has gifted me with ALS. While life is full of difficulties, pain, and suffering, there is so much to be grateful for. While I understand the hardships, I choose to focus on the positive parts of my life and that keeps me going. There is my wife, my children, family, and friends. And even within the suffering and difficulties I can still contribute and help others. Through my blog I have the opportunity to learn and teach Torah. I forged new friendships with the teens and yeshiva boys that visit. Being crushed has brought stronger connections, new abilities, higher purpose, and deeper meaning. I've been blessed with a voice that can't sing and with a body that doesn't work. So I dance to a new rhythm. I'm Yitzi Hurwitz, and I know that I matter.[10]

Then, on the eighth and seventh levels, he connects his spirituality to the values of patience, kindness, and wisdom. On the sixth level, he sees himself as a balanced and discerning adult who deals with life's challenges with balance and fortitude (identity). This level of self-perception then leads to levels 5a and 5b towards forming positive beliefs; both in terms of how he views himself as being a capable individual, and in his positive relationship with others.

With this new sense of optimism, on the fourth level, he spends less time in thinking patterns such as negative filtering. On the third level, his thoughts are positive, unburdened, and focused. On the second level, he is happy and content *in spite* of the progression of his illness. And on the first level, he behaves with dignity, approaching his situation with patience, knowing that eventually everything will work out for the good.

Thinking Slower to Go Faster

There are unique individuals like Rabbi Yitzi Hurwitz or Jerry Long who choose to live life from a higher perspective. They were able, with significant mental exertion, to overcome inescapable predicaments. Others who struggle with chronic depression or anxiety may be too consumed with negative thinking patterns to access higher levels of thinking.

In the next chapter we will explore the steps needed to accomplish this psychological transformation. The first step is the psychological approach of Rabbi Dovber, the Mitteler Rebbe, who describes how to focus your mind to access higher levels of thinking. The second step is by focusing on positivity and staying solution focused.

Takeaways

- Thinking on higher levels accesses powerful emotional resources that exist beyond, but also within, the self.
- Higher spiritual values cascade downwards and influence all of a person's thoughts, feelings and behaviors.
- According to Viktor Frankl, D=S-M means that Despair equals Suffering minus Meaning. When you add meaning to your suffering, you avoid despair.

Questions for Self-Exploration

- When facing an emotional crisis, try thinking about God and see what happens to your emotional reality.
- What is the real purpose of your life?
- What good things can you focus on right now as opposed to the bad?
- What emotional resources, memories, and values can you meditate on to change your emotional well-being?

CHAPTER 5:

The Mitteler Rebbe and the Psychology of Losing Your "Self"

"Don't aim at success. The more you aim at it and make it a target, the more you are going to miss it. For success, like happiness, cannot be pursued; it must ensue, and it only does so as the unintended side effect of one's personal dedication to a cause greater than oneself or as the by-product of one's surrender to a person other than oneself."
—Viktor E. Frankl, *Man's Search for Meaning*

What if the most important breakthroughs in therapy have come not from the world of psychology, but from spiritual wisdom and guidance? Over 200 years ago, almost a century before Freud and the advent of modern psychology, the "Mitteler Rebbe," Rabbi Dovber Shneuri (1773–1827) explained in his writings that a person who strives to live on an optimal emotional level needs to not focus on himself but beyond himself.

Interestingly, Viktor Frankl also cautioned against self-focus, which he called "hyper-reflection."[1] Hyper-reflection, he maintains, can be seen when someone obsesses too much about himself, which only tends to increase his neurotic symptoms. For example, ironically, a person who excessively worries about having a panic attack can actually *trigger* the anxiety he aims to avoid. Hyper-reflection and its symptoms can also be witnessed in popular culture that promotes "selfies," full expression of a person's individuality, and plastic surgery, yet statistically sees increasing rates of depression, anxiety, and despair. The modern obsession with the self has not improved people's lives.

Frankl's answer to hyper-reflection is what he calls "de-reflection." This means taking the focus off of yourself and de-reflecting onto some tasks or meaning to fulfill. In other words, you need to first "lose yourself" to find who you really can become. An example of de-reflection is from a transcript of Frankl's advice to Anna, a 19-year old art student who displayed severe symptoms of schizophrenia. She considers herself confused and asks Frankl for help.

Patient: What is going on within me?

Frankl: Don't brood over yourself. Don't inquire into the source of your trouble. Leave this to us doctors. We will steer and pilot you through the crisis. Well, isn't there a goal beckoning you— say, an artistic assignment?

Patient: But this inner turmoil . . .

Frankl: Don't watch your inner turmoil but turn your gaze to what is waiting for you. What counts is not what lurks in the depths, but what waits in the future, waits to be actualized by you. . . .

Patient: But what is the origin of my trouble?

Frankl: Don't focus on questions like this. Whatever the patho-logical process underlying your psychological affliction may be, we will cure you. Therefore, don't be concerned with the strange feelings haunting you. Ignore them until we make you get rid of them. Don't watch them. Don't fight them. Imagine, there are about a dozen great things, works which wait to be created by Anna, and there is no one who could achieve and accomplish it but Anna. No one could replace her in this assignment. They will be your creations, and if you don't create them, they will remain uncreated forever. . . .

Patient: Doctor, I believe in what you say. It is a message which makes me happy."[2]

Surviving on a Death March

Frankl himself de-reflected in Auschwitz when he transcended his own existence to stay alive. On one occasion while emaciated and placed on a death march, if he would show himself to be weak, take a break, or fall he would instantly be shot by a Nazi guard. Suddenly at the moment of near collapse, he de-reflected and focused on a higher meaning:

A thought transfixed me: for the first time in my life, I saw the truth as it is set into song by so many poets, proclaimed as the final wisdom by so many thinkers. The truth—that love is the ultimate and the highest goal to which man can aspire. Then I grasped the meaning of the greatest secret that human poetry and human thought and belief have to impart: The salvation of man is through love and in love. I understood how a man who has nothing left in this world still may know bliss, be it only for a brief moment, in the contemplation of his beloved. In a position of utter desolation, when man cannot express himself in positive action, when his only achievement may consist in enduring his sufferings in the right way – an honorable way

– in such a position can, through loving contemplation of the image he carries of his beloved, achieve fulfillment. For the first time in my life, I was able to understand the meaning of the words, "The angels are lost in perpetual contemplation of an infinite glory."[3]

The Five Psycho-spiritual States of Rabbi Dovber

Remarkably, Frankl's allusion to the angelic contemplation of God and His infinite glory is similar to what Rabbi Dovber described in *Kuntres HaHitpa'alut* (*Tract on Ecstasy*). In this extraordinary work, Rabbi Dovber defined five states of spiritual contemplation that lead a person away from oneself. Accessing these five states depends on a person's ability to dereflect from the "self'" and to contemplate solely on God's presence. By losing himself, and attaining a state of flow during contemplation, a person moves away from his materialistic self toward his higher Godly self.

By way of analogy, imagine you hear a voice in the room next to you and you are intrigued. Is it the voice of a radio that someone forgot to turn off? Is it the voice of someone speaking to someone on the phone? At the same time you are trying to make out what is in the room, you hear some noise outside, making it even harder to hear what is happening inside the room. However, as you get closer to the room it becomes progressively clearer that the sound is a human voice. Each step you get closer to the room you get further from the distracting noise that is outside. And, as you approach the room, you begin to hear who is speaking and eventually you can hear exactly what they are saying.

Rabbi Dovber describes the experience of achieving these five progressive spiritual states of awareness by focusing primarily on God's omnipresence. Each step closer is one step away from yourself, and one step closer to something greater.

The five stages are:

1. Nefesh (body): Belief, and acknowledgment of a truth
2. Ruach (emotions): Emotion, as an inspired fantasy and anticipation of an expected outcome
3. Neshamah (thoughts): Understanding, true feelings in the heart
4. Chayah (superficial unconscious): Inner focus and passion
5. Yechidah: Simple Will or "Identity"[4]

A person progressively climbs the ladder of these states when they think deeply about God. The more engrossed they become in meditation, the higher they go. However, Rabbi Dovber cautions us that there is a preliminary state to the five aforementioned which is the person's desire for his "personal experience" hindering his ability to lose himself. This is what Frankl refers to as "hyper-reflection," where a person focuses primarily on himself, even if this is for his own spirituality. According to Rabbi Dovber, "this is not Divine excitement at all, because he does not desire or intend any aspect of Godliness whatsoever. His intention and goal is not that Godliness dwells in his soul or that his soul be bound to Godliness etc., but rather to have something of a thrill, so that he can be aware of his self-existence."[5]

Imagine a person trying to meditate just to feel the thrill or pleasure of the meditative experience. Paradoxically, the desire to achieve meditative ecstasy could be masking an excessive focus on the pleasure state that arises in meditation (rather than focusing on the object of meditation). This person's ulterior motive is to "feel himself" on a spiritual level through contemplation, or to experience his own greatness through meditation. The challenge here is that if the person hyper-reflects on his need for personal experience or emotional growth, this separates him from the object of meditation, which is to experience God.

Rabbi Dovber calls this "a completely strange fire." At this stage, "there is no meditative concept of God at all, only in the most general way."[6] The initial motivation is still driven by the need to fulfill the self-directed drive for spirituality. He has not yet transcended "hyper-reflection" even in spiritual terms. He is still in a state where he desires "self" actualization which, again, falls short of "losing the self" in something greater. According to Rabbi Dovber, he wants to "feel" himself in his meditative experience.

Stop Trying to Relax

As a therapist, I often see this phenomenon when a client who is suffering from anxiety or pain asks me for a technique to calm down his nervous sensations. I usually suggest that they gently focus on their tense bodily sensations and simply describe them to themselves in their mind's eye. For example, when a person feels a knot in their stomach, due perhaps to some anxious thought, I have them notice what they are feeling and simply describe it to themselves. After a few moments of contemplation, most sensations inevitably dissipate. However, there are some clients who say, "I'm trying hard to notice it, but it doesn't seem to relax." I tell them that "I didn't say you should try to relax. Rather, I want you only to *notice* it."

When a person "intends" to relax, usually the opposite occurs. However, when the focus is on simply *describing* the sensation without an ulterior motive, i.e. relaxation, ironically the client's sensations will gently dissipate without much effort. So too, in this first contemplative state of Rabbi Dovber, the person is working on noticing God and less about their spiritual needs.

The first stage that follows the preliminary state is "Belief, and acknowledgment of a truth." Here a person is now trying to connect to God and to become aware of His presence in the world. However, the matter of Godliness is still distant from him and is tainted by a false spirituality that still involves a sense of the "self." Here, the person is now focused on God but still wants to feel this consciously, thereby losing the vitality of the connection. According to Rabbi Dovber,

> There is some hidden admixture of good here which comes from the aspect of the concealed love of God within his heart. That is, it is hidden within the alien garment of his revealed desire. Nevertheless, all this notwithstanding, in a hidden way, his essential desire is specifically to become excited about HaShem and if it would not be about HaShem, he would not want to pursue it altogether.[7]

The second stage is called "Emotion, as an inspired fantasy and anticipation of an expected outcome." This is the love and fear of God as they relate to action only. Here one longs for this Divine subject to be fixed firmly in his soul, in the category of "open experience." The person's objective is that he wants to be close to God but has not yet attained this level. It only exists as an "intellectual acknowledgement" without any automatic love or excitement.

At the second stage of thinking about God, love and fear are not as yet actually felt in the heart. However, they are present in sufficient strength to create a resolve to do good. As Rabbi Dovber explains:

> This level is better than the previous one because, at least, it is close to arriving at actual Divine excitement. This is because, after all, the contemplation of Godliness is important to him. He greatly desires it and his chief goal and desire is to approach it. Only that though he occupies himself with it, he does not affect Divine excitement from it in his heart and mind at all. However, it is not for his selfish pleasure, but solely for Godliness, since his only desire is that closeness to God be firmly established in his soul.[8]

The third stage is called "Understanding, true feelings in the heart" and can be likened to a person engrossed in a business deal where he stands to profit. As the deal inches closer to finalization, he becomes increasingly moved on an emotional level. So too, when thinking about connecting to God, the individual commits the entire power of his mind to "adhere to this thought with an excitement called adhesion of the thought (strong attachment of thought in that he is greatly affected and moved by it). The indicator for this is that he becomes preoccupied and moved (absorbed and engrossed).[9]

To explain this stage, Rabbi Dovber quotes from the Torah concerning the directive to recite the Shema:

> The verse states, "And you shall love with all your heart" which means with both your good inclination and your bad inclination. In Hebrew, the word heart is usually spelled with one "Beis." Here it appears with two beises, therefore signifying two sides of the heart, both good and not good. This is the essence of the commandment to serve God with the "heart" which specifically means to be excited. This occurs due to the fact that as soon as a good thing arises in his thoughts it excites his mind and emotions in a revealed way."[10]

The fourth stage occurs when a person meditates to the point where it brings about an immediate and spontaneous emotional excitement in his heart. This state is known as "Inner focus and passion" (superficial unconscious), and it "brings about an immediate and spontaneous emotional excitement in his heart, in an aspect of an excitement that is felt with a greater and more inner vitality than the intellectual excitement, mentioned above."[11]

Think for a moment of a scientist who believes he has found the secret to a new scientific discovery that could change the world. He throws his mind entirely into the subject, forgetting to eat, and he barely sleeps for days on end. Here the person is fully engaged in accomplishing a task or fulfilling a goal with all his heart. This high level of concentration and dedication to a cause creates power momentum in a person's life where they have forgotten themselves and are fully engrossed at helping others, improving society, or changing the world around them. At this stage there is no space for self-reflection. Selflessness and determination run the individual's life.

Full Absorption

The fifth stage is known as "Simple will" or the "Identity." It emerges as a result of intense contemplation, to the point that a person becomes even higher than being "fully excited in his heart." He can see the essence (in one glance) of what he is contemplating upon, which in this case is God, in Whom he is fully absorbed. He experiences himself as if he is "before HaShem" and that "everything is as nothing" except God's wholeness.[12]

Rabbi Dovber maintains that this level of self-transcendence is achievable through deep contemplation, which leads to a loss of the self, enabling "ecstasy" (full absorption) to follow. He describes this psychological phenomenon as akin to the exhilaration experienced with a melody, where a person spontaneously becomes excited and loses themself in the song:

> By way of example, this may be understood from the spontaneous excitement of great joy that a person has when very good news reaches him. Certainly, the excitement could be so strongly felt in his heart that he may make strong automatic and involuntary gestures, such as clapping his hands. This takes place without choosing or intending it. Rather, he claps involuntarily, automatically, and this, itself, is the indicator that he is not at all aware of himself being excited, though it is felt in the heart. However,

it is as if he is totally unaware of it. This is because it is genuine excitement resulting only from the good thing itself that his soul is bound to. He then does not at all feel his excitement, because he never intended to become excited. Rather, the excitement is automatic, so much so, that he can be completely unaware of it. This is also similar to what we observe in the opposite emotion; that when a person is angry, he is neither aware of nor does he feel his excitability, etc.[13]

This highest level is similar to what Frankl noted as the fullest expression of the *religio,* which becomes fully manifested and is the essence of a total selfless experience, which Rabbi Dovber compares to the awareness that *"before God, everything is as nothing."*

Practical Application

Let's apply this in psychological terms. Take a person who focuses solely on a topic that brings them great pleasure. Imagine a person thinking about an idea that would possibly influence their life positively, like building an extension to the back of their home. At first, they think about adding a room jetting out into the backyard. Then, they imagine themselves walking into the room and seeing the light pouring in from the windows. They progressively start to fill in all the parts of the picture, including the furniture, the lighting, and the colors on the walls. Next, they envision their family members and loved ones in the room. Eventually, their imagination is fully absorbed in the sensations of being in that room and enjoying it with family. They have moved from "hearing from afar" (Rabbi Dovber's first level) to fully experiencing the "essence" of the intended object, until they feel "as if" they were actually sitting in it.

Another example would be a mathematical problem through which a person fully engages all of their intellectual skills and meditates upon it for long periods of time. At first, they are aware of their own inadequacies, and they are concerned that they cannot accomplish the task. They then continue to delve into the equation and, without being aware, they become fully engaged in the topic and forgets themself. The person loses touch with time, hunger, and other responsibilities. Hours later, the phone rings and wakes them from their contemplation. They realize that time has passed, they have skipped dinner, and they need to run out to go shopping. They were able to forget themself for the sake of the matter at hand. Some may refer to this as a flow state. This person was able to fully "de-reflect" and experience something beyond themself.

A New "DSM"

Unfortunately, as therapists, we tend to focus more on the "negative" aspects of our clients and do not provide a counterbalanced view of what a positive life looks and feels like. A perfect example of the over emphasis on negativity is the manual we use to describe mental illness called the DSM.

The DSM stands for the Diagnostic and Statistical Manual of Mental Disorders published by the American Psychiatric Association (APA). It lists descriptions of mental health conditions ranging from anxiety and mood disorders to substance-related and personality disorders, dividing them into categories such as major depressive disorder, generalized anxiety disorder, and narcissistic personality disorder.

For each category, the manual includes a list of diagnostic criteria, which are symptoms and guidelines that health professionals use to determine whether a patient or client meets the criteria for one or more diagnostic categories. For example, the current DSM states that to diagnose depression, a person "shows at least five of a list of nine symptoms (including depressed mood, diminished pleasure, and others) within the same two-week period." It also requires that the symptoms cause "clinically significant distress or impairment in social, occupational, or other important areas of functioning," along with other stipulations.

What is missing in the DSM are categories of mental wellness which are calibrated with one's level of meaning and corresponding with positive emotional states. However, with the psychology of Logotherapy and the description of states of "de-reflection" and acquisition of meaningful thoughts outlined by Rabbi Dovber, we may now form a new diagram of emotional dysfunction *and* resilience.

	State	Description	Emotions
0	Foreign Fire	Depression, Anxiety	Sadness, Fear
1	Nefesh (body): Belief, and ac-knowledgment of a truth.	Interest	Pleasantness
2	Ruach (emotions): Emotion, as an inspired fantasy and anticipation of an expected outcome.	Desire	Delighted
3	Neshamah (thoughts): Un-derstanding, true feelings in the heart.	Spiritual Arousal	Captivated
4	Chayah (superfi-cial unconscious): Inner focus and passion	Engrossment	Joy
5	Yechidah: Simple Will or "Identity".	Ecstatic	Euphoria

Instead of simply undoing the negative states of emotion with our clients, we can now describe these states to them and help them find more meaning. These higher states are the antidote for feelings of depression and anxiety.

In other words, instead of focusing on the past and a person's negative experiences, we can focus on the possibilities of what a life looks like when one is de-reflecting towards higher goals and realities. The goal would not be to simply remove his or her feelings of sadness or fear, but to focus on helping them to experience feelings of interest, desire, spiritual arousal, being engrossed, or in a state of ecstasy. In Logotherapy, we presuppose the existence of these positive levels and help our clients draw closer to them by focusing on the acquisition of finding more meaning in life.

How to De-reflect

For most people, however, it is very difficult to become fully engrossed in matters outside of themselves that cause them to experience such profound personal transcendence. Most oscillate back and forth between experiencing ourselves intermittently while we are connected to other people, places, and things.

To taste and experience the psychological benefits of de-reflection, I created a simple guided meditation to help my clients go "beyond" themselves.

Here is a script for the meditation:

1. Think about all of your faculties of seeing, hearing, tasting, smelling and touching. Imagine waking up in the morning and feeling as if you were granted a new day in your life. You notice that your eyes are able to see, your ears are able to hear. You become aware that your heart is beating, you are breathing, and that your mind can perceive many wonderful

thoughts. You are thankful for all of the miracles of your body that give you the strength to move, lift, and protect yourself.

You recognize that all of this comes from God, who gave your mind the ability to distinguish between day and night. He allows you to see, picks you up from what burdens you, gives you clothing to wear, strengthens you when you are tired, and takes care of your needs.

. Think about the gift of life itself. That you were born and fed, and you were taught how to speak, write and to understand the world around you. Contemplate all the things you actually have in your life:

- Electricity to turn on lights
- Water to drink
- Shelter
- Transportation

Reflect on the most basic items in your home and the thousands of individuals who made those things possible and made your life more pleasant:

Now, take a moment to reflect on all the thousands of people who have worked hard, some without knowing you at all, to make your life easier or more pleasant.

- Farmers who grew your food.
- The truckers who transported food to your supermarket.
- People who work in your local stores or online.
- Your letter carriers, sanitation engineers, and workers

who provide you with water, electricity and gas.

- Remember that you barely know any of these individuals, yet they are improving your life every day.
- Fill your mind and heart with gratitude for everything you have and what you own.

2. Now, notice all your resentments: people you are angry at; those who let you down; and individuals you are angry at but you cannot do anything about it. Let all of those resentments go. Allow your greater self to emerge by becoming humbler. See yourself, not as the center of the universe, but as a small part of a greater whole. You were given everything you were supposed to have. Nothing has happened by accident. Everything you need was prepared for you your entire life. Give up your feelings of ego, jealousy, anger, and disappointment. See yourself as serving a higher purpose and not just in terms of your own demands and needs.

View each resentment as an opportunity to allow God into your life. Let Him release you from all of your disappointments and anger. Feel the power of letting go and just being a vehicle or bringing a higher will into your life and into the lives of others.

3. Think about your purpose in life. What is your unique mission to fulfill? What values do you ultimately stand for? Compassion, Love, Kindness, Justice? Contemplate what kind of human being you want to be and be responsible for your vision of the highest "you" possible.

4. Contemplate that before the world existed there was only God. Then He decided to create the world by emptying a

small space within Him so the world could exist. He then entered His light into the empty space and progressively concealed his light to the degree that it seemed as if He had disappeared, knowing that He was only concealing Himself within the physical and spiritual worlds

All of this was done to allow you to exist and to sense your "independence" to make your own choices. He wants you to reveal Him in the world through your acts of kindness and goodness, and via your fulfilling His commandments. He created you with all of your abilities to be His partner in co-creating a world where He can dwell through the choices you make and your behaviors.

Become God's partner in recognizing His oneness in the world by saying twice daily: "Hear o Israel, the Lord our God, the Lord is one." Think deeply about this stanza, and when you say the word "one," imagine His dominion reaching over the four corners of the world expressing His unity.

5. Now see yourself as a vehicle for bringing His blessings in the world. Wish goodness to people in your life: family members, friends, partners at work, community members and those in your city and country. Extend this even to those you dislike.

   Use words to bring blessings of peace, joy and completeness to those you are close to. Think about the needs and wants of people around you and ask that their needs be fulfilled. Notice those who are poor, sick, or unable to take care of their needs and help them with your words and your actions. See yourself on a mission to transform and elevate the world.

Step aside from your own needs and focus on taking care of others and improving their lives.

Remind yourself throughout the day that your mission is to "give yourself over to a higher power," serving goals and a purpose beyond yourself.

Paradoxical Intention

Frankl created another technique to lose oneself called Paradoxical Intention. It consists of persuading a patient to engage in something they fear. It operates on the idea of recursive anxiety, which is also known as fear of fear.[14] Paradoxically, as they intend to trigger their feared sensation, they are unable to and therefore realize there is nothing to fear.

One example is the fear of public speaking or having sweaty palms in social situations. According to Frankl, we ask the client to trigger the sensations they are having until they see the futility of their fears. When they are able to see the ridiculousness of their obsessive thoughts, they can move onto fulfilling more important tasks in their lives, such as focusing on the quality of the lecture and not on their fears about it.

Paradoxical Intention is based on the concept of systematic desensitization, which involves "gradually exposing a person to something that causes extreme fear and panic and teaches them to replace fear responses with a relaxation response."[15]

According to Cocchimiglio (2022), a protocol to induce Paradoxical Intention would be to ask the four following steps:

1. Find ways to make the experience bigger, heightening their emotional response.
2. Place themselves in the situation rather than avoiding it. For example, if the client fears failing, they place themselves in situations where they are likely to fail.

3. Repeat the process until the idea of failing (or any other fear) no longer fills them with anxiety and dread.[16]

In a case where the public speaker fears that their heart will race, we ask them to purposefully try to make their heart race. Paradoxically, when they try to increase their heart rate they see that it doesn't work. This can also be applied to sweaty hands, fears of passing out, wobbly knees, stomach aches, etc.

The Power of Humor

Finally, Frankl speaks about the power of laughter and how humor comes into play. Discussing how he survived in the concentration camps Frankl explained the role humor played in his ability to "de-reflect" and ultimately to survive:

> To discover that there was any semblance of art in a concentration camp must be a surprise for an outsider, but he may be even more astonished to hear that one could find a sense of humor there as well; of course, only the faint trace of one, and then only for a few seconds or minutes. Humor was another of the soul's weapons in the fight for self-preservation. It is well known that humor, more than anything else in the human make-up, can afford an aloofness and an ability to rise above any situation, even if only for a few seconds.

> The attempt to develop a sense of humor and to see things in a humorous light is some kind of a trick learned while mastering the art of living. Yet it is possible to practice the art of living even in a concentration camp, although suffering is omnipresent.[16]

In conclusion, these brief techniques—such as Paradoxical Intention and humor—help a person lose focus on the "self." They thereby dereflect and create the emotional "space" needed to shift their orientation, and free them to explore new possibilities beyond themselves as we will learn about in the next chapter.

Takeaways

- Waiting deep inside your psyche is a *religio* that wants to connect you to a higher state of spirituality.
- Gratitude, Letting God in, Visions, Oneness, and Blessings are powerful tools to shift away from yourself to higher realities.
- Describing states of being—as opposed to trying to force a change—helps you enter into a contemplative state of mind away from anxious and depressive thoughts.
- Engage your mind in spiritual concepts to become fully absorbed in a state of flow with your higher aspirations.
- If you have a fear of a certain situation, by trying to trigger the anxiety response, intensely, paradoxically, you can reduce recursive anxiety.

Questions for Self-Exploration

- Has focusing too much on yourself made you less depressed or anxious?
- How do you feel while focusing on "being happy"? Does focusing on achieving happiness make you happier? Or does it feel better to aim for fulfilling goals and values where the by-product is a state of happiness?
- What type of ideas, meditation, or contemplation help you to think beyond yourself? Gratitude, thinking about God's oneness, etc.

CHAPTER 6:

Spiritual Contemplation in Psychotherapy

**"Between stimulus and response, there is a space.
In that space is our power to choose our response.
In our response lies our growth and our freedom."
—Viktor E. Frankl**

The desire to find meaning or to maintain a spiritual focus may be hindered by a person's symptoms of depression or anxiety. Those who struggle emotionally often feel overwhelmed with negative thoughts or disturbing sensations (racing heart, headaches, sweaty palms). Powerful feelings hijack their ability to de-reflect or think on higher levels.

In therapy with my clients who struggle with their emotions, I help them to first slow down their thoughts by reflecting upon *what* they are thinking. In psychology, this is known as metacognition or "thinking about thinking" and self-reflection.

Frankl spoke about the need to self-reflect and create "space" from your thoughts when he stated: "Between stimulus and response there is a space. In that space is our power to choose our response. In our response lies our growth and our freedom." When we exercise this mental control, we have "space" to transcend our thoughts, as described in the following diagram:

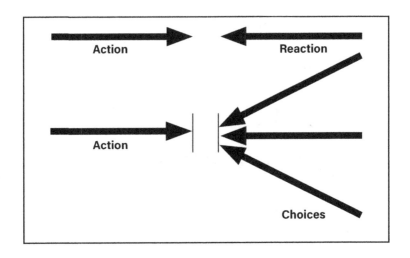

SPACE DIAGRAM

The top diagram shows a typical reaction to a stimulus, i.e., someone pushes you, or you have an anxiety-producing thought. In this case, stimulus (the push or the thought) is followed by an emotional reaction (pushing back or feeling anxiety). In the top diagram, you are reacting automatically to someone or something that bothers you.

The bottom diagram introduces the space between the stimulus and the response. According to Frankl, that space gives us the power to choose how we react. Detaching and watching ourselves think is the first step in this direction.

Here are a few questions you can ask yourself to practice metacognition:

- "What am I thinking about right now?"
- "How do I usually respond in a situation like this? Are there other ways of responding?"
- "What information am I missing that would help me make this decision?"
- "How do I know what I think I know right now? Can I be truly certain about this?"

For those who find it hard to slow down their thoughts, I have them begin by taking a deep breath and just thinking about their thoughts without judgment. If you are doing this now, just notice your thoughts without judgment. Are they racing or slowly moving through your mind? Are your thoughts flowing or do you feel stifled? Do you notice any patterns?

The Power of *Iyun*

As you enter a metacognitive state your thoughts slow down and it's easier to focus. Metacognition may even change your brain waves, creating an overall sense of calmness and inner peace. Feeling calmer gives you the "space" to deeply focus your mind on more productive thoughts, which is a process called, in Hebrew, *iyun* (pronounced "*ee*-yoon") or in-depth study.

In his writings on meditation, Rabbi Dovber (the Mitteler Rebbe, Rabbi Dovber Shneuri, also mentioned in chapters 1 and 4) explains that *iyun* transforms your mind and brings you into higher states of awareness inaccessible when your thoughts are scattered. *Iyun* is achieved by "gazing strongly into the depths of a concept, keeping one's mind upon it for long periods, until he understands it thoroughly in all of its particular parts and details."[1] When the mind is deeply focused on the matter at hand, one can access higher levels of understanding and awareness.

In contrast to mindfulness, where a person "empties out" his mind, *iyun* is achieved through the full engagement of one's consciousness. In-depth study is also the opposite of what is defined as "surface study." Rabbi Dovber explains that:

The explanation of surface study is that one understands the subject matter only at first glance. That is, he moves quickly through the subject matter that he studies, without restraining himself and pausing at all, as known. For example, one may gaze upon a certain object without contemplating it at all, to understand the nature of how or what it is. He does not investigate all its inner and outer parts, except in a passing fashion.[2]

Going Deeply Into Your Thoughts

Iyun implies going beyond superficial layers and getting to the depth of the matter. In therapy, I have my clients "do *iyun*" on their own thoughts. *Iyun* enters them into a state of self-contemplation where their prefrontal cortex (analytic brain) is fully engaged in understanding itself.

I have witnessed a phenomenon that by simply having my clients focus on their thoughts, they then enter into a state of "flow" that is defined as a cognitive state where one is completely immersed in an activity. Psychologist Mihaly Csikszentmihalyi describes "flow" as "a state in which people are so involved in an activity that nothing else seems to matter."[3] It can be witnessed when artists are engrossed in their paintings, musicians are playing their instruments, and when someone is thinking deeply about a topic which may include one's own thoughts.

Length, Width and Depth

In the *Tract on Contemplation,* Rabbi Dovber describes how a person can enter into this state of contemplation (*iyun*) by utilizing three aspects of thought: length, width, and depth. Length is the concretization of a person's thoughts. Rabbi Dovber explains that it is the "tremendous descent of the concept, to invest it into various different analogies so that it may even be brought within the reach of a small child."[2]

In psychological terms, we aim to elicit from our clients various analogies or thoughts they have about any topic. By doing so, we help them concretize what they are thinking by helping them bring their thoughts to the forefront. Rabbi Dovber explains that, like "a flowing river that draws out to its length,"[4] so too a person's mind maintains many thoughts they may have about any given topic. And when they are expressed, they become more concretized on a conscious level.

Questions a therapist would ask to elicit "length" of a person's thoughts would be, "What are some examples of when you get panic attacks?" or "Does it happen when you walk down the street?" or "Can you give me any other instances where you have felt scared in other scenarios?" Common responses would include: "I feel scared when I go to a wedding," "I also feel scared when I go shopping in the mall," and "Sometimes I feel panicked when I'm left alone in the house." The more concrete examples the client is elicited to share, the more "length" they are giving to their thoughts.

The next step is to bring "width" to a person's thoughts by helping them explore and analyze them from different angles. This process is similar to finding "width" in a river as opposed to a "narrow" stream where there is very little flow. To "broaden" a person's thoughts, the therapist asks questions such as "It seems that you are afraid in different situations. You mentioned it in public, at malls, and at home. In what ways are they similar or different?" or "What do you think these many thoughts are telling you? Essentially, what do you think they are all about?"

When a person contemplates long enough on his thoughts from different angles, he begins to uncover "depth." Depth will be noticed especially when a person has an "Aha!" moment, where his different thoughts suddenly uncover a hidden theme, the "depth" of the problem.

Meditative Moment. Did you ever think deeply about a topic or feeling, and it helped you understanding yourself more clearly? Sit for a moment contemplating an emotional predicament. As you seek out interconnected patterns of thoughts notice what insights emerge.

Rabbi Dovber explains that:

The depth of a concept is analogous to the depth of a river. From its depth the river widens, but in and of itself it is not wide at all. However, it [the depth] is the main essence of the river (which is called the "undercurrent"), for it is the main strength of its flow from its source. The waters which are above the depth, to its height or its sides and even its length, are secondary to the depth, for they only represent the spreading forth of its strength. Likewise, the depth of the intellectual concept is the aspect of its essential point, as it is in and of itself. This is what is called "the depth of that which is comprehended" (*Omek ha'moosag*).[5]

Einstein and Finding Depth

One example of how contemplation reveals depth is that of Einstein's *Theory of Special Relativity*. After contemplating for long periods of time the nature of various forms of matter in the universe (length) and contrasting and comparing all of the scientific theories of the universe (width) from many different angles, Einstein was able to reveal its essence, that energy and mass are correlated as explained by the equation "$E=MC^2$" (depth).

In psychological terms, "depth" perception occurs through sustained contemplation until a flash of insight reveals the source of one's thoughts. For example, a person who panics when his spouse is away, thinks deeply about his fears of being alone, suddenly remembers that in third grade he came home one day, and the door was locked. As he slows down his thoughts, he recalls banging on the door until he realized that his mother was not home. He then remembers crying and thinking that something bad had happened to her and suddenly felt that he was abandoned.

He also recalls that about half an hour later his mother suddenly arrived home looking distressed and rushed to comfort him. Although she explained that her car broke down and she couldn't reach him, the damage was done, and it left a deep impression in his nervous system that he was abandoned and perhaps may be abandoned again in the future.

Now, looking back with a deeper awareness of his fears, he understands *why* he panics even years later while being in a big crowd, or even while being at home alone. In actuality, anytime he feels alone, he experiences an overwhelming sense of powerlessness, and his body goes into a panic state that he cannot easily shake off or ignore.

If he goes even further he may also discover that there were many times when his mother was available for him and that his trauma was an exceptional occurrence. When he focuses on all the loving support he received from his mother, he then finds new and positive and supportive emotional resources, which become the springboard for his recovery.

How Rapid Changes Occur

After years of helping my clients contemplate their thoughts, I'm still amazed each time I witness how quickly change takes place. This is not something a therapist can force. It is the outcome of calm and focused contemplation, where the client creates an inner flow of ideas and arrives at his own depth of understanding.

The therapist cannot push a client in this direction. Rather, the therapist gently guides the client to slow down their thinking patterns and analyze their thoughts (from different angles), and the therapist assists them in exploring these different areas in the client's mind. As their thoughts slow down, this gives space to the client's positive and spiritual inclinations that stream into their consciousness, bringing awareness about the nature of—and solutions to—their problems.

Contemplating on Higher Levels

I often think about the metaphor of a person digging for water in a field. If they dig deep enough, long enough and in the right place, suddenly water comes gushing up to the surface. As we keep on digging down even further, we then discover what Frankl calls "the unconscious God." This is a powerful experience when a person comes in contact with their higher spiritual yearnings and sense of purpose.

By employing the three types of thinking (length, width, depth), a person uncovers their higher levels of meaning (especially levels seven and above relating to meaning, values, spirituality, and purpose) and their inherent connection with God. Here, the therapist is simply removing the impediments that were keeping the spiritual unconscious concealed until they burst into consciousness.

Meditative Moment. Sit quietly with the thoughts that emerge in your mind. Then notice what other thoughts appear. Contemplate the connection between them and the essential message they are teaching you. Watch and see what thoughts emerge.

Maps of Meaning

Here is a step-by-step list of questions that can take a person from their initial thoughts, emotions, and sensations to ascend up the "ladder" towards more meaning.

Level 1 (Behavior/ Sensations)	Length	Width	Depth
	What is the problem?	In what ways is this challenging for you? Which areas of your life does it affect?	Do you see a pattern here?
	What's happening right now?	When else has this occurred?	What do you think is the core issue?
	What are you feeling in your body right now?	Where else do you feel sensations? Can you compare those sensations? Are they the same, different, etc.?	Where do you feel the sensations are coming from?
Level 2 (Emotions)	Length	Width	Depth
	What emotions are you feeling right now?	What other feelings are you having?	What's the earliest memory you have of this feeling? What is this feeling saying to you? What do you really need?
Level 3 (Thoughts)	Length	Width	Depth
	What are you thinking about?	What are your other thoughts about this issue?	When is the earliest memory of these thoughts? Is there a pattern in your thoughts? What does this remind you of in your life?

Level 4 (Thinking patterns)	Length	Width	Depth
	In what ways are you looking at the problem? Are you engaging in black-and-white thinking? Are you magnifying your mistakes? Are you minimizing your accomplishments?	Are you applying this thinking pattern to other circumstances?	When did you start thinking like this? During childhood or after a specific trauma? Where does this thinking pattern come from?
Level 5a (Beliefs/Self)	Length	Width	Depth
	What do you really believe about yourself?	Does this (belief) apply in other areas of your life?	Do you believe you are worthless, helpless, or unlovable? Where does that come from?
Level 5b (Beliefs/Others)	Length	Width	Depth
	What do you believe about that person? (the person who hurt you)	Are there other behaviors that bother you about that person?	Did you experience any similar traumas with them (or others) when you were younger? Where does that belief come from?
Level 6 (Identity)	Length	Width	Depth
	How do you view yourself? (Protector, Nurturer, Victim?)	Does your self-image affect other areas of your life? In what ways (positively or negatively)?	How did you develop that perception of yourself and your role in life?

Level 7 (Meaning)	Length	Width	Depth
	What is meaningful to you?	What other areas in your life do you find meaning in?	What is the highest area of meaning you can detect? Where do your perceptions of meaning come from?
Level 8 (Values)	Length	Width	Depth
	Which values are important to you?	Are there values that are in conflict with one another?	What is your highest value? What is the source of your value?
Level 9 (Spirituality)	Length	Width	Depth
	What is really important to you spiritually? What is your true purpose in life?	Can you think of other instances in which you lived with or without your spiritual values? How did that affect your life?	What is your highest spiritual value? Where does that come from?
Level 10 (Spiritual Essence)	Length	Width	Depth
	What is your personal relationship like with God?	In what ways has your relationship with God influenced your life?	When you contemplate that your soul is a part of God, in what ways does that affect your thoughts, emotions and behaviors?

Level 1: Behaviors/Sensations

We begin with questions on the first level, which lead you to self-reflection and to greater awareness of the root cause of your problem(s).

On level one we begin by exploring your physical sensations that you are currently feeling. Questions include: "What are you feeling in your body right now?" (length) and we continue exploring this sensation by asking, "What else are you feeling in your body right now?" We then proceed to create more "width" by asking, "What's the difference between this physical sensation and the other ones?" Finally, we create more "depth" by asking, "What is this feeling saying to you?" or "What is the sensation telling you need right now?"

Level 2: Emotions

Level two questions focus on the feelings associated with your sensations. For example, "What are you feeling right now?" (length). This is followed by width-oriented questions, such as "Have you ever felt this way in other situations?" or "What are some other feelings you have had that are similar to these?" And finally, we focus on discovering depth by asking, "What's the earliest memory in, or about, which you have a feeling?" or "What is this feeling saying to you, what does it want from you?"

Level 3: Thoughts

At level three (thoughts), we ask, "What are your thoughts on the matter?" and "What are you thinking about in the situation you are in currently?" (length). We then expand to width-oriented questions such as "What are your other thoughts about this issue?" or "In which ways are your thoughts on this issue different from other issues you may have had in the past?" We then move on to depth-oriented questions such as "When was the earliest time you remember thinking thoughts like this?" or "Is there a pattern in your thoughts that you can connect together?"

Level 4: Thinking Patterns:

At this point in the session, as the client explores his or her thoughts, their mind begins to slow down as they start to see the interconnectedness of their thought patterns. On the fourth level one becomes aware of their misplaced thinking patterns (level 4) that may be the source of unpleasant emotions. Length-oriented questions on this level include "In what ways are you looking at this problem?" or "Are there certain negative thought distortions that you are continuing to use (i.e., black-and-white thinking, negative filtering, overestimating danger, etc.)?"

In terms of width, we then compare these thoughts with questions like "How are these patterns being utilized in different areas of your life?" or "How is this affecting you in other circumstances?" And finally, we explore "depth" with questions such as "When did these patterns start?" or "What was the source or memory that is causing you to look at life from such a perspective?" or "What do these patterns of thoughts remind you of from your childhood?"

Level 5a: Beliefs/Self

At level 5a we uncover beliefs about ourselves. Examples of length-oriented questions include "What do you believe about yourself?" or "What is that saying about how you view yourself?" Width on this level is expanded by comparing self-beliefs by asking: "Does this belief apply to other areas of your life?" and "What do the differences in your beliefs mean to you?" And finally, to assess the depth of your thoughts we ask, "Deep down inside, do you believe you are worthless, helpless, or unlovable?"

Level 5b: Beliefs/Others

Beliefs about others (level 5b) are often a reflection of our own self-beliefs. For example, if we believe we are weak, we tend to believe that others are more powerful than us. If we consider ourselves unlovable, we are critical of other people and find it hard to treat them kindly. Length-oriented questions include: "What beliefs do you have about the person (or thing) that is bothering you?"

Width-oriented questions explore different ways one perceives other people's behaviors, such as "Have there been other times where you believed 'x' about people?" Finally, when we arrive at depth analysis, we explore the origin of one's beliefs by asking: "Are your beliefs based upon previous traumas when you were younger?" or "What do you assume about most people? Do you believe they have your best interests in mind or that they are deliberately trying to hurt you?"

Meditative Moment. Contemplate your self-beliefs. Do you have different beliefs that may be in conflict? How do you view yourself? Are your beliefs negative, or are they positive in nature?

Level 6: Identity

Beliefs are often formed by our identity (level 6). They are a reflection of how you view yourself and have formed your self-concept. Identity may be positive or negative and the implications are significant. You may view yourself as a protector, nurturer, or healer. Conversely, you may see yourself as a victim, hero, loser, or outcast, etc. This will deeply influence your self-beliefs, thoughts, emotions and behaviors. For example, if you view yourself as being a leader in your family, you can more easily assert your needs at home. If you view yourself as a victim, you may cower when confronting a difficult sibling.

Length-oriented questions that stimulate a discussion about identity include: "How do you view yourself?" and "Who do you identify as a role model?" We then delve into your thoughts about your identity (width) by asking, "Does your self-image affect other areas in your life? In what ways, positively or negatively?"

Finally, we expand depth by asking, "How did you develop that sense of yourself or your role in life?" and "Where does your identity

94

come from? Is it a response to trauma, a challenge in your life when you were younger, something you watched or were told?"

De-reflecting beyond Yourself—Level 7: Meaning

Once we have arrived at level seven (meaning), we now shift from self-reflection (the first six levels) to what Frankl calls "de-reflection," or reflection away from yourself.

Focusing on meaningful behaviors helps you to actualize your values and participate in meaningful activities (i.e., studying a new language, helping others, learning Torah, or playing an instrument). Length-oriented questions at the seventh level include: "What is meaningful to you?" and "What can you carry out with your life right now that is important to you?"

We then progress to help the person explore the width of their thoughts, by comparing and contrasting different levels of meaning, such as "What other areas in your life do you find other types of meaning?" and "In what ways are they similar or different?". Finally, we proceed to explore the highest levels of meaning by asking, "What is ultimately meaningful for you?"

Level 8: Values

On the next level (level 8) we explore your values. Length-oriented questions that stimulate awareness of the eighth level include "What values are important to you: honesty, kindness, compassion, etc.?" and "What are some values that you would like to actualize including creative, experiential and attitudinal values?" and "Is there something you could do with your skills that is important to you? Is there someone you could love more authentically? Is there something you could experience in the world that is meaningful, like nature, culture, learning, etc.?"

We then deepen the discussion by asking width-oriented questions such as "Are there other values that are in conflict with one another?" For example, a person who honors the value of truthfulness can feel conflicted when his colleague asks him to comment on whether he likes the colleague's new car. On the one hand he wants to be truthful; on the other hand he wants to be kind. By asking width-oriented questions, we compare and contrast your values, which will help you to see a pattern. Questions that elicit this information include: "What is your highest value?" and "Where do your values come from?"

Ultimate Meaning—Level 9: Spirituality

According to Frankl, at the highest levels we arrive at thoughts relating to "ultimate" meaning or spirituality. On the ninth level we probe into the spiritual dimensions of your life. Length-oriented questions about spirituality include: "What is really important to you spiritually?" and "What is your true purpose in life?" and "How important is spirituality to your life right *now*?" as well as "What experiences have most shaped your spiritual life?"

We broaden the discussion with width-oriented questions such as: "What experiences have you met with or without your spiritual values and how did that affect your life?" and "How do these spiritual values compare?" and "In what ways could spirituality help you overcome your suffering/challenges?" We then ask a depth-oriented question, such as "What is your highest spiritual value?"

Level 10: Spiritual Essence

There are times, however, where even spiritually-oriented questions are not powerful enough to help you find the relief you are seeking. For example, there are those who face situations of inescapable suffering, such as facing terminal disease, loss, or a disability, and they need to reach the highest level of their existence.

Existential questions (questions about existence) uncover the highest depths of your soul. They move you towards contemplating your relationship with the Creator. Length-oriented questions that arouse this awareness include: "What is your personal relationship like with God?" or "In what ways has your relationship with God influenced your life?"

Width-oriented questions include: "Do you experience God in a positive or negative light?" and "What did you learn growing up about God that affected your view of Him?" and "Looking at the different experiences you've had in your relationship with your personal connection with God, what have you learned?"

We then help you explore the "depths" of your spirituality by asking, "When you contemplate where your soul came from, in what ways does that affect what is ultimately meaningful to you?" and/or "How would that level of spirituality affect your thoughts, emotions, and behaviors?" And finally, we ask, "In what ways can your inherent connection with God change your life?"

The Cause of Emotional Eating and Obesity

Here are two examples of how I put Rabbi Dovber's psychology into practice with my clients. Several years ago, Sarah, a 53-year-old mother and preschool teacher, came to speak to me about her obesity. Her doctors were concerned that her cholesterol numbers were too high and that she was in danger of heart disease. She was desperate to lose weight and despite her efforts to do so, she continued to gain more. Sarah believed she had an eating addiction, stemming from the stress of her son's disabilities.

After meeting with numerous physicians, they suggested that Sarah speak to a therapist to discuss her emotional eating patterns. I used Rabbi Dovber's approach to help Sarah resolve her eating issues arising from her relationship with her son. At our first meeting, I guided Sarah to deeply reflect on her own thinking patterns to find the source of her emotional eating:

DS: So what is the problem you want to work through today?

Sarah: I want to lose weight.

DS: So, what would you get out of losing weight? How would your life be better?

Sarah: Probably wouldn't be in this much pain and could do a little bit more. I'd be healthier.

DS: Okay so you'd be in less pain and get to do more and be healthier. That makes sense. So, what has stopped you previously? Sarah: I think it's my guilt. I've used it as self-punishment, and, because of the years of caring for him, I've damaged my body as well as my back.

DS: So you mentioned that you're covering up some sadness and some guilt. Can you tell me more about that?

Sarah: Well the guilt that my son has a genetic disease. What he has even though I'm not a carrier, was a spontaneous genetic mutation. But I blame myself for him and having that for the rest of his life and I blame myself.

DS: So you believe it was your fault? (Sarah pauses a reflects)

DS: I understand. I'm just wondering, what has that got to do with your current weight situation? Tell me more about the guilt. What does your guilt have to do with losing weight? . . . Just spend a moment and think about your thoughts. . . . Slow it down and think about the question: What does guilt have to do with your eating patterns?
(Sarah's eyes look glazed as she turns her head upward towards the right and stares off into her imagination. Around 30 seconds of silence follows as she goes into a state of deep self-reflection).

Sarah: I think, yeah, well, that I'm responsible. But I also know that it's probably nothing.

DS: So maybe, or probably?

Sarah: I'm not sure. Maybe I've turned it into something.

DS: You've *turned* it into something. . . . Just think about how you did that. . . . Think about how you've turned it into something.

At this point I simply reflected and amplified Sarah's own beliefs that she had turned something unrelated to overeating into chronic obesity. When I helped her slow down her thought patterns she became even more introspective. This helped her enter a state of inner contemplation which led to her uncovering more profound connections.

In Sarah's case, at first, she was unsure of why she had a problem with emotional eating. Only through slowing down her thoughts and guiding her to think in depth about them was she able to examine the source. In her case it was that she maintained the belief that she was responsible for her son's illness.

Other common examples can be seen when clients present with anxiety and report that they are suffering from panic attacks, especially when they are left alone, but they have no idea why they feel this way. The goal of the therapist is to help the client concretize or "lengthen" what she is thinking by assisting her to express as many examples as possible to clarify the nature of the panic attacks.

This occurred with Sarah when I had her focus on the purpose of being a parent.

DS: And so, how are you feeling about your relationship with your son at the moment?

Sarah: We have a good relationship. It's really about me being a good mom.

DS: What's that like, being a good mom? [Here I help Sarah reflect on the higher value of being a loving "mom" to her son.]

Sarah: You know, taking care of a child is a mom thing. As a mom, you always worry you can never go away, can't go away.

DS: Because that's to do with being a mom. You worry that he won't have the best life possible, correct?

Sarah: Yeah, I do, I worry that he can't have the best life that he can. It's just normal, normal to see what's happening there.

DS: What are you curious about?

Sarah: What's normal?

DS: It seems that you are normal, wanting the best for your kids and worrying about them.

Sarah: Right. It's for wanting the best for the kids and worrying about them.

DS: And that is normal as a mom.

Client: Yep. I Know.

DS: So I wonder what we can learn from that: for yourself and for you personally.

Sarah: What can we learn from that? That everything I was doing was normal.

DS: Yes. You were doing the best you could. That was your purpose, to be the best loving mom possible. That was normal, right? It was just being a good mom.

Sarah: I was normal.

DS: It was more than normal. It is your purpose.

Sarah: Yes, it's one of my most important values. First, and the second is my children.

DS: How does it feel to know that you are living with your values?
Sarah: When you put it that way, it is much better.

At this point Sarah began to realize that she had no reason to feel guilty. Instead, she is comforted, knowing that she has always lived authentically as a loving mother to her son. Her values have been to be a good mom and to live a spiritual life. And it is this newfound clarity and sense of purpose which can help her reduce her feelings of guilt and her emotional eating as she focuses on the positive role she plays in her son's life.

Meditative Moment. What is the misplaced thought you have about yourself that is causing you emotional pain? What positive thought can you replace that with to heal yourself?

Additionally, once we uncovered her purpose and meaning to be "a good mother," we could use that to change her eating patterns. We could reframe her eating habits in terms of her greater purpose: to be the best possible mother to her son, she would need to be present and as healthy as possible. She could accomplish this through viewing each meal as an opportunity to nourish her body and nurture her son, rather than punish herself through food to cope with her guilt and sadness.

A Case of Abuse and Recovery

Next, let us take the case of Shlomo, 21, who suffered extreme abuse from his father. When he was a child, he would frequently be beaten or attacked for even the slightest mistakes. Ever since, he was plagued by feelings of insecurity and low self-esteem and often suffered from depression and anxiety attacks. He was, however, a shining personality and no one would guess the significant suffering he endured. He was smart, hard-working, and a pleasure to speak to. Although he had so much going for him, he suffered internally, feeling that he had no place in this world and no inherent value.

Shlomo had already been in therapy for several years suffering from PTSD. He had previously tried EMDR, a type of therapy which focuses on exposure to one's traumatic memories, through utilizing various eye movements. He reported that he did not feel better from his last round of therapy treatments. I decided to use Contemplative Therapy to help Shlomo think on a higher level and feel better about himself.

One day, Shlomo sent me a message, via WhatsApp, about rescheduling. I noticed that Shlomo's WhatsApp picture was of him wearing a crown as a child. I asked Shlomo what that represented to him:

DS: I noticed that you were wearing a crown in your profile picture. What does that represent to you?

Shlomo: Despite what I experienced, I always viewed myself coming from royalty.

DS: What's that royalty all about?

Shlomo: My mother once had a dream that she was the descendant of a king. I grew up believing that to be true, and it gave me at least a fantasy, to pretend it was true.

DS: Yes. How does kingship make you feel about yourself?

Shlomo: I am really a king in many ways. It affects the way I dress, talk to others and relate on dates. Despite what I went through, then and now, I believe I have something higher within me. It's like a sense of higher purpose, like I didn't sink fully into the world of my abuse. I can always rise above it when I see my own image as a king.

During the subsequent session, I asked him about what he felt was the most important value of his life. He told me that despite his pain, he deeply believed that God created him to be kind to other people, to heal others' emotions, and to succeed in his studies.

I asked him to contemplate for a few moments the self-perception of his royalty that he was the son of a great King and that he was given a unique mission that no one else besides him could ever accomplish. As he meditated on that thought for several minutes, I noticed that his body language started to shift. He began to sit up with more confidence. A small smile broke out on his face, and he started to relax. Shlomo was accessing and focusing on a higher vision of himself, which helped him begin to regulate his thoughts and emotions and start feeling better.

What I have discovered is that a person's higher perception of him or herself, and their spiritual thoughts, can be buried deeply in their unconscious mind. Positive thoughts have been secreted away, repressed from years of invalidation, neglect, or abuse. However, when you meditate on higher perceptions of yourself and find exceptions to the way you now perceive yourself, you have the freedom to choose a different pathway without limitations.

Takeaways

- In order to heal your emotions, you first need to think about how you are thinking.
- A person needs to look at the length, width, and depth of their thoughts.
- Deeply reflecting on your thoughts allows you to see their interconnectedness.
- Thinking from level seven upwards allows you to access new and powerful emotional resources.
- The more you focus on achieving pleasure, the more pleasure is elusive.
- Focus on the self is called "hyper-reflection," which can be rectified by "de-reflection" or reflecting away from oneself.
- Choose values and goals to fulfill you, and happiness will ensue.
- Spiritual states are more accessible when you focus less on yourself and devote your time and energy to a higher cause.
- Try the four-part meditation daily, and observe how changing your perspectives changes your thoughts, attitudes, and behaviors.

Questions for Self-Exploration

- If you spend a moment contemplating your thoughts, what do you notice?
- If other thoughts arise, when you compare and contrast them to each other, what do you begin to understand about yourself?
- Do any deep insights emerge from your contemplative experience?
- What did you learn about yourself that can change your attitude towards life?

- What could you accomplish if your spirituality were fully actualized? Would you give more charity, feed hungry people, perform acts of kindness, pray for longer periods of time, or read and complete more spiritual texts?
- Imagine a marriage, family etc. bringing you tremendous happiness. What would be happening in your home?
- What would a fulfilling spiritual life look and feel like?

CHAPTER 7:

The Power of
Solution-Focused Therapy

"A positive attitude enables a person to endure suffering and
disappointment as well as enhance enjoyment and satisfaction. A
negative attitude intensifies pain and deepens disappointments; it
undermines and diminishes pleasure, happiness, and satisfaction;
it may even lead to depression or physical illness."
—Viktor E. Frankl, *Man's Search for Meaning*

So far, you have learned some new ways of thinking. You have learned
that searching for meaning and discovering your own unique life's
purpose can be powerful resources to help you rise above the lows
in your life. Now, it is time to change the way you see yourself entirely.
This is the second most important principle of Logotherapy: to focus on
your positive parts, and not on the negative. This can be accomplished
by focusing on "exceptions."

"Exceptions" are those ideas, thoughts or beliefs that are different
from what you consciously believe about yourself or focus upon. Exceptions shift the focus onto the positive parts of the self, the good things
you have done, your positive desires, and the right choices that have
brought you to where you are today. Exceptions are the antidotes to
many thinking traps, especially Negative Filtering.

Rabbi Nachman on Seeing Only the Good

Rebbe Nachman of Breslov taught us to look for "exceptions" in ourselves and in others. He sourced this idea to a cryptic stanza in the book of Psalms that reads: "And in yet a little bit and the wicked is not; and you will contemplate on his place, and he is no more" (Psalms 37:10).

According to Rebbe Nachman, this means that although a person feels badly about themself, if you help them explore a "little bit" beyond their negative thoughts, you will find the good. And, when you contemplate with them about their goodness, they are no longer in their place of negativity, meaning they have transformed their self-image.

> **Meditative Moment: What is a "good" part of yourself that is being repressed? Try to focus on a positive aspect of your personality and see how that makes you feel.**

Psychologist Dr. Barbara Fredrickson, a key researcher in the field of positive thinking, also believes that increasing positivity and finding "exceptions" is the key to overcoming emotional distress. She maintains that the best way to reduce anxiety is by arousing positive emotions like love, joy, and gratitude. And she contends that a positivity/negativity ratio of 3:1 must be maintained to experience the benefits of positive thinking. This means that you have to "crowd out" your negative thoughts with more positive exceptions.

Fredrickson developed a method to increase positive thinking using "Positivity Portfolios"[1] to develop a person's capacity for happiness. The portfolios contain photographs and mementos of the people, places, and things that generate a heartfelt feeling of positivity. The ten portfolios Fredrickson suggests are joy, gratitude, serenity, interest, hope, pride, amusement, inspiration, awe, and love.

Fredrickson's system works like this: Let's say that in the "joy" portfolio you collect pictures, or you write down notes about all the joyful moments in your life, like the birth of a child, a birthday party, graduation day, a wedding, etc. In the "gratitude" portfolio, you make a list of all the people you feel grateful for. You read through your portfolios a few times a day to increase overall positivity, especially at times when negative thoughts occur. The portfolio helps you shift toward and focus on positive thoughts to awaken feelings of happiness.

In Logotherapy we ask our clients to develop their positivity portfolios as we focus on their "exceptions." This contrasts with questions that only probe negative emotional experiences, such as a person's causes for their depression or anxiety. What you focus on determines the outcome of the discussion.

Here are some of the solution-focused questions we ask, to create a positively-focused session:

Looking Forward

- What can we work on that would make the most difference for you?
- What's going on in life that has your attention right now?
- What do you want more of in life? What do you want less of?
- If you really got radical today, stopped fearing the consequences, and set out to become what you were born to be, what would you be doing?
- Tell me about a big dream that you've always wanted to go after.
- What would be most helpful to focus on right now? It could be an upcoming decision, a practical challenge you face, a transition, a dream: you name it.

Leaving Things Behind

- What is getting in the way of living the life you want?
- What do you want to accomplish?

- If one burden could be removed from you in the next thirty days, what would that be?
- If you could wave a magic wand and change one thing about your life, what would that be?
- Where are you stuck or not moving forward? What is stymieing your progress?

What Is Already Working for You?

- In which ways are parts of your dream already coming true?
- What has helped you to achieve similar goals?
- What did you do the last time you were faced with such a challenge?
- How did you manage to do that?
- What other examples come to your mind?
- What else?

What Is Right about You?

- What has happened to you positively since we met last week?
- What are some of the successes you had since we spoke last?
- What's right about you?
- Despite the mistakes you made, what did you do right?
- You mentioned that you got angry at your colleagues at work last week: When were you kind to them?
- Tell me about some of the acts of kindness you have done over the years towards others.

These kinds of questions lead to finding exceptions from their negative perceptions of themselves. When you do this successfully, you arouse a positive energy that affects the entire session and influences what clients think about themselves between the sessions.

The Case of the Oddly-Shaped Ear

One example of exploring a client's "exceptions" occurred unexpectedly in a session with Chani, age 29, who was suffering from trauma from her abusive marriage. During a discussion about her childhood and self-esteem issues, she mentioned that kids used to bully her about her oddly-shaped ear. It turned out that several individuals in her family shared the same genetic characteristics and had undergone plastic surgery to change their appearance. She, however, refused to have surgery for her ear.

I was curious about how she was able to confidently live with this characteristic, which her siblings could not tolerate. I wondered what level of thinking she was utilizing to achieve her positive level of awareness. She explained that these genetic similarities could be traced to her grandmother's ears that had the same unique feature. She loved her grandmother, and associated only positive and spiritual qualities with her and would never change her own ears. Chani was able to find the good in what would be perceived by others as a blemish. What emerged was that her oddly-shaped ear was actually a reminder of her grandmother that connected her to her kindness and values.

Through Logotherapy, this woman was able to expand her awareness and to find meaning in spite of what she considered a clear and visible physical blemish. This was accomplished by finding the "exception" to others' limited ways of thinking and believing. She was able to transform what others viewed as a negatively-associated birth defect (the likeness of her grandmother) into a positive and powerful force in her life.

**Meditative Moments. Is there a part of you that you reject?
What thoughts or beliefs do you associate with your
"imperfection". What positive thoughts, meanings
or beliefs can you associate with it instead?**

Finding Exceptions to Depression

Other examples of finding exceptions occur when clients report feeling depressed for long periods of time. After delving into their history about the symptoms and severity of their depression, I also explore ways in which there have been exceptions to their depressive symptoms. In seeking exceptions, we ask the question, "During this time, were there ever times when you have *not* been depressed, or perhaps less depressed?" Many will report that there have been several times where they felt less depressed. For example, when they visited a good friend, exercised, went on vacation, or had a fun trip.

Once we understand a person's exceptions to their symptoms, we focus on magnifying them by asking questions such as "How can you spend more time visiting friends, exercising, or taking vacations?" and "What's stopping you from doing activities that bring you joy?"

As Rebbe Nachman explained, once you focus a person away from the negative place where you originally met him, "he is no longer there," meaning that he is now in a different place. This is because our positive exceptions have the power to energize us to *move* in their direction and to accomplish even more. When we focus on the good, as opposed to the bad, our minds expand. We are energized with a new impetus to continue our emotional growth and healing.

Consider the case of Mark, a 40-year-old client who struggled with low self-esteem and bouts of depression. Early on in my sessions with Mark we searched for his "exceptions":

DS: So what exactly do you want to work through? Give me a bit of an idea to find out what exactly it is?

Mark: I'm feeling down and depressed. I feel like I lack self-confidence.

DS: I see. Are there times you don't feel as depressed or more confident? [Exceptions]

Mark: Yes. When I do the things I like, and enjoy, I feel more confident and happier. Like when I'm playing music, I feel less depressed.

DS: Anything else?

Mark: I love boating in summer and try to spend my weekends canoeing down the Delaware River.

DS: When was the last time you did that?

Mark: Last summer I went canoeing with my son and his best friend.

DS: Tell me more about that.

Mark: We had a great time. We went at the end of August when there weren't so many bugs out, and the weather was perfect. The kids had a great time portaging with the canoes from place to place and spending hours going down the river. The best part was camping at night and making a fire. We had a great time.

DS: Thinking about going down the river and having a great time, what are you noticing in your body?

Mark: I'm feeling a sense of warmth in my arms, and my chest and in my heart.

DS: Excellent. Stay with that. Tell me what you notice.

Mark: It feels nice, like waves of sensation.

DS: Is it happier and more confident?

Mark: Yes, I would say so.

DS: So, when else are you more confident?

Mark: While playing music.

DS: What do you play?

Mark: Guitar.

DS: Imagine yourself playing right now.

Mark: Ok

DS: What do you feel?

Mark: The same feeling.

DS: Stay with that.
(The client closes his eyes and then tears up.)

DS: What just happened?

Mark: I started feeling something very enjoyable. It feels like something spiritual, like I was praying.

DS: Nice. What does it feel like when you're praying?

Mark: I feel as if my full body gets lifted up with the music.

DS: Just continue to stay with that.

Exceptions work because individuals tend to dwell on what's wrong with them—as opposed to what's right with them. In Logotherapy, we always assume the best about our clients and merely facilitate them becoming more aware of who they truly are or want to become.

Takeaways

- Try focusing on the positive and not the negative.
- Seek out exceptions to your negative memories and beliefs about yourself.
- If you're feeling depressed, ask yourself about times you were not depressed and what you were doing then. Then, do more of that.

Questions for Self-Exploration

- What is the ratio of your positive to negative thoughts?
- What are the exceptions to your negative beliefs?
- What are you doing when you feel good?
- Look for the "exceptions" in other people as well and see how that makes you feel towards them.
- What state of being do you want to arouse? Happiness? Joy? Success?
- If you could become radical and dream about something you want to accomplish (even if it seems impractical) what would that be?

CHAPTER 8:

The Neuroscience on How Thinking about God Changes Your Brain

"Religious and spiritual contemplation changes your brain in a profoundly different way because it strengthens a unique neural circuit that specifically enhances social awareness and empathy while subduing destructive feelings and emotions."
—Andrew B. Newberg, *How God Changes Your Brain: Breakthrough Findings from a Leading Neuroscientist*

How does thinking about God affect your brain? For over a decade I have been working with clients who reported feeling better when they accessed their spiritual longings, found new meaning in their lives, and connected with God in a profound and personal way.

The positive results I have seen are significant. Not only were my clients able to make changes in their thinking patterns, but they were also able to *maintain* those changes by continuing daily spiritual practices that enhanced their feelings of emotional well-being.

Here is some of the feedback clients have reported to me after concluding therapy:

- "I was struggling in therapy for years trying to figure out why my father never really loved me. It was only when I started focusing on *me* and my current passions in life that I started feeling better."

- "I was molested by a family member many times when I was a child and teen. My therapist kept pushing me back to open up my trauma, but that just made me feel worse. I enjoyed how you stayed focused on the positive within me. Since we first met, I started exercising and after many years of being a stay-at-home mom, I just started looking for work again."
- "The more my first therapist started opening up my beliefs about myself, the worse I felt. I appreciated how you kept me focused on being a better person and fulfilling my passions. Thank you so much!"

These comments, and many others, have reinforced my belief that Viktor Frankl's insights into the human condition were correct. Often therapy doesn't have to dig down deeper, it needs to teach people to climb higher.

How Thinking about God Can Change Your Brain

In my previous book, *Think Good and It Will Be Good,* I discussed a study by Dr. David Rosmarin, a professor of psychology at Harvard Medical School, that demonstrated that spiritually-focused therapies such as Spiritually-Integrated Treatment (SIT) performed just as well if not better than other therapies such as Progressive Muscle Relaxation (PMR), which is a standard relaxation technique used to treat anxiety. The study took two groups of clients who struggle with anxiety and provided one group with PMR and the other with SIT (i.e., increase faith in God). SIT participants reported greater results.

Rosmarin's extensive research has shown the connection between increasing trust in God and reducing anxiety. His study entitled,

"Spiritually-Integrated Treatment," found that treating anxiety with a faith-based intervention for thirty minutes a day over a two-week period, was more effective than traditional forms of therapy.[1] Based on *Duties of the Heart*, by Rabbi Bachya Ibn Pakuda, the intervention includes the following exercises:

- Introduction about the purpose of the program (to increase trust in God)
- Inspiring anecdotes about belief
- Reading four passages from Torah sources about belief
- Picturing a person you trust and imagining that he/she was sent by God to help you
- Thinking about a precious item and trying to imagine that God sent it to you
- Thinking about a stressful time in the past that turned out better than expected, and then contemplating God's role in the event
- Thinking about God's role while engaging in physical activity (standing up, lifting, etc.)
- Praying for help to increase trust in God

The study required participants to read inspiring stories highlighting trust in God and how stressors and obstacles may be blessings in disguise. Participants were asked to read teachings of *Chazal* (rabbinical stories) about trust and belief. Additionally, they used guided imagery to envision someone they trusted being sent as a messenger to provide help, as well as to generate appreciation for something important in their life. Finally, the participants spent time thinking about how things had turned out better than expected during stressful times in their life. They learned to attribute positive outcomes to God's benevolence, and prayed to increase their trust in God, so that things would turn out well for them in the future.

The study found that SIT participants showed significantly reduced levels of stress, worry, and symptoms of depression from following the prescribed regimen. They also reported "greater belief in treatment credibility, greater expectancies from treatment, and greater treatment satisfaction than PMR participants." The SIT group improved in their ability to tolerate uncertainty, which leads to an overall reduction in anxiety, compared to the Wait List Control Group [those who did not receive any therapy].[2]

The Neuroscience of Spiritual Thinking

Rosmarin's work demonstrates the results of spiritually-focused therapy through observation of his clients' behaviors and verbal attestations to the efficacy of his protocols. But what is occurring internally can perhaps only be studied through neuroscience. Due to advances in fMRI technology, neuroscientists can view what is actually happening inside people's brains when they think about God.

To begin with, we already know that positive thinking has been scientifically found to actually change a person's brain structure. For example, Dr. Susumu Tonegawa and his colleagues, at the Center for Neural Circuits Genetics at the Massachusetts Institute of Technology, studied (in mice) how positive experiences change how the brain works. In their lab, mice overcame chronic stress by reactivating neurons that had been used during positive experiences (like being with a mate) to prevent depressive behaviors.

Dr. Tonegawa's research showed that the hippocampus, a structure of the brain that changes in response to stress and depression, also responded to positive thoughts. Stress reduces the generation of new neurons in the brain, making it vulnerable to depression. However, reactivation of neurons that had been active during a positive experience restored neuron development in the hippocampus and reversed the effects of depression.[2] In other words, the process of activating positive thoughts is enough to restructure the brain to reduce anxiety or depression.

Positive thinking also has been shown to change a person's brain chemistry by elevating serotonin levels, which play a vital role in the development of depression and anxiety. A study in the *Journal of Psychiatry and Neuroscience* recruited actors who were able to maintain intense memories of either positive or negative experiences.[3] The actors underwent brain scans when they were focused on happy thoughts and memories. The scans showed that their brains increased the production of serotonin, which reduces depression and anxiety. However, when the actors focused on negative memories, serotonin levels in the brain decreased, showing the connection between thoughts and brain chemistry.

To juxtapose the influence positivity has on the brain, let's compare what the average child or teenager in our society experiences while he is playing video games. In an article titled "Video Games on the Brain," Lyla Patel found that there are some main areas of the brain that may be positively affected by playing video games such as the premotor and parietal cortex, dopamine, and gray matter. Certain games can improve motor skills, speed up rates of thinking and reacting, and increase logical thinking. Playing can also stimulate dopamine receptors in the brain to increase feelings of pleasure.[4]

However, the positive aspects are greatly overwhelmed by many of the negative effects that occur in the brain, which may include the shrinking of the underside of the frontal lobe which causes mood alterations. This leads to increased moodiness, anxiety, and aggressiveness, which may occur even after the conclusion of the game itself. In terms of the amygdala, which regulates the fight-or-flight mechanism, frequent play of violent, aggressive video games leads to symptoms of increased anxiety and aggressiveness.

Many other studies clearly demonstrate that where and what you focus your mind on affects how you feel and behave. Those who spend time focusing on positivity, as opposed to violence or mindless activities, show a significant difference in brain activity, emotion regulation, and mood stabilization. If we take this to the next therapy session, when we meditate on God and the ultimate "good," what happens from a neurological perspective?

What Happens To Your Brain When You Think About God?

Researchers Beauregard and Paquette at the University of Montreal were interested in studying what happens to the brain when a person thinks about and feels the presence of God in their life. To do so they took fMRI images of the brain to see what occurs. The images suggested that those who have what they define as a "union with a higher being that accompanies religious experiences" increase electrical activity in parts of the brain that govern feelings of "peace, happiness, and self-awareness"[5].

Using the brain scans of fifteen individuals, they discovered electrical activity and blood oxygen levels had surged in at least twelve regions of the brain. The regions most affected by "religious experiences" were the medial orbitofrontal cortex, which is connected to emotions, and the right middle temporal cortex "which is believed to be responsible for the impression of contacting a spiritual entity."[5] It is important to note that in these areas of the brain, heightened activity plays a major role in the treatment of depression, anxiety, and PTSD.

Neurotheology

What effect does just thinking about God have, and how can this practice help individuals with depression, anxiety, or PTSD? In a new field called *neurotheology*, neurologist Andrew Newberg, M.D., has been researching what happens in people's brains when they are in a deep spiritual state while meditating or praying, finding meaning, or simply thinking about God.

In his groundbreaking book, *How God Changes Your Brain*, Newberg reported that when someone has a spiritual experience or thinks about God, different circuits in the brain become activated, while others become deactivated. Deactivation of parts of the brain like the amygdala (a part of the brain that regulates anxiety) is also very important. When the amygdala is active, a person experiences heightened sensations of anxiety, which floods the body with adrenaline, raises blood pressure and pulse, and causes muscles to tense. Other times, new and important synaptic connections are made, and the brain becomes "more sensitive to subtle realms of experience."

Newberg believes that if connecting to God is a focus of your mind, then it becomes neurologically noticeable, and you will alter your neural circuitry more significantly. In a nutshell, Newberg discovered that:

1. Each part of the brain constructs a different perception of God.
2. Every human brain assembles its perceptions of God in uniquely different ways, thus giving God different qualities of meaning and value.
3. Spiritual practices, even when stripped of religious beliefs, enhance the neural functioning of the brain in ways that improve physical and emotional health.
4. Intense, long-term contemplation of God and other spiritual values appears to permanently change the structure of those parts of the brain that control our moods, give rise to our conscious notions of self, and shape our sensory perceptions of the world.
5. Contemplative practices strengthen a specific neurological circuit that generates peacefulness, social awareness, and compassion for others.[6]

Newberg maintains that living a religiously and spiritually focused life enhances "cognition, communication, and creativity, and over time can even change our neurological perception of reality itself." For example, one of his studies measured changes in blood flow in the brain during "verbal"-based meditation involving the internal repetition of a particular phrase (i.e., Shema Yisrael "Hear, O Israel, the Lord our God: the Lord is One). He found that, compared to the brain flow before meditation, scans showed an "increased blood flow in the prefrontal cortex (7.1%), inferior parietal lobes (6.8%), and inferior frontal lobes (9.0%)."[7]

In another study he also found that the cerebral blood flow of long-term meditators was "significantly higher compared to non-meditators" in many parts of the brain which also affected the "attention network and also those that relate to emotion and autonomic function"[8]. The autonomic nervous system regulates symptoms of anxiety and depression and is often the focus of somatic therapy in the treatment of PTSD.

Meditative Moment. Take a moment to contemplate on a spiritual or universal thought. How does that impact your heart rate and tension levels? Does it bring you to a greater state of calmness?

Greater Impact than CBT or Psychoanalysis

What's even more significant is that unlike other forms of therapy such a CBT or psychoanalysis, thinking about God does not just affect one part of the brain, it affects several different regions. These brain functions include "holistic, abstractive, existential, and emotional components" and each of these functions can be generally attributed to different brain areas.

Let's look at a model of the brain to understand how it works.

Our ability to see, for instance, is controlled by the occipital lobe, which processes vision and images. The parietal lobe is a part of the brain that is responsible for detecting sensations. It is only behind *that* that we are able to notice objects. In the front lobes of the brain (frontal cortex), abstract thinking and planning are more prevalent.

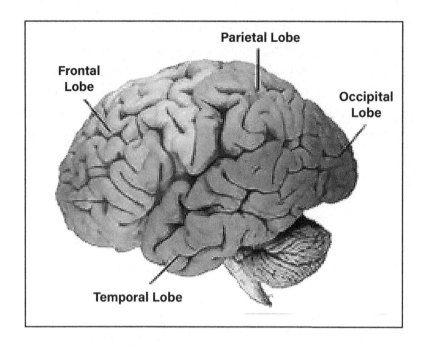

According to Newberg, the frontal cortex of the brain, which provides us with logical and rational thinking, can allow us to see God acting in the world through various laws and principles. The middle brain, or what is known as the limbic system, creates for us an emotionally meaningful experience of God. Other parts of the brain are associated with different experiences of God. For example, the occipital cortex, which is at the back of the brain, helps us envision an anthropomorphic perception of God (God as a father, protector).

When activated, the parietal lobe gives us a sense of time, space, and other objects in the world. The parietal lobe is also affected through spiritual practice. It has been shown that reduced electrical activity in the right parietal lobe, a structure located above the right ear, is associated with self-transcendence, increased consciousness, alertness, and the ability to understand other people's feelings and thoughts. This, according to Newburgh, can help us conceptualize a God and His oneness in the universe.

Additionally, the ability to become connected to something higher than oneself lasts even beyond the time of meditation. This suggested to Newberg that meditation, over time, strengthens one's sense of self in relation to the world and other spiritual dimensions.

Finally, another part of the brain affected by spiritual thoughts is called the anterior cingulate cortex (ACC). This part of the brain mediates between the front of the brain, which includes the logical brain; and the middle brain, which includes the limbic system or emotional brain. The ACC is involved with social awareness and intuition, allowing a person to feel more empathy for others. Meditation and spiritual practices stimulate activity in the ACC, therefore helping a person to become more sensitive to the feelings of others.[9]

Spirituality and Neurotransmitters

Newberg's research also uncovered the connection between spiritual practices and neurotransmitters, which are the chemicals that make your brain work. For example, those who practice daily meditation were found to have a 65% increase in dopamine.[10] Dopamine heightens our ability to imagine things, generate pleasurable experiences, stimulate positive thoughts, and to feel more safe in the world. According to Newberg, the ability to believe in spirituality may be dependent upon the dopamine that is released in the front of the brain. And his studies showed that during meditation, serotonin is released, which has been shown to decrease depression and reduce anxiety.

Additionally, Newberg demonstrated that those who perform spiritual meditation have an increase in GABA levels in the brain by as much as 27%, which is also associated with low levels, depression, and anxiety.[11]

Long-Lasting Impact of Spirituality

One of the most important conclusions Newberg makes is about how spiritual thinking creates a lasting impact on the brain. In one study, he worked with older individuals who were experiencing memory problems. After taking scans of their brains, Newberg taught them a mantra-based type of meditation and asked them to practice that meditation for twelve minutes a day during an eight-week period. After a follow-up scan, he found some significant differences, especially in the areas of the brain that helped them focus. The participants reported improved memory and the ability to think more clearly.[12]

Spiritual Feelings and Inner Peace

One of the more interesting studies on spiritual practice found that deep spiritual thinking activates the "same reward-processing brain circuits as sex and other addictive activities."[13] Research led by researcher Dr. Jeff Anderson, Ph.D., from the University of Utah School of Medicine in Salt Lake City, examined the brains of nineteen young Mormon students using an fMRI scanner.

The students were asked about the intensity of their religious experience. Those who reported a sensation of "feeling the spirit," which implied being spirituality engaged with intense spiritual feelings, displayed "increased activity in the bilateral nucleus accumbens, as well as the frontal attentional and ventromedial prefrontal cortical loci." These are pleasure and reward-processing areas of the brain that are also activated when we engage in sexual activities, listen to music, etc. The participants also reported feelings of "peace and physical warmth."[13]

These findings also corroborated other studies that found that engaging in spiritual practices raises levels of serotonin, which is the "happiness" neurotransmitter. It also raised their levels of endorphins, which are the natural opioid related painkillers in the body.

Seemingly, research is showing only positive benefits from being spirituality focused. The benefits include clarity in one's thoughts, resolved cognitions, and having overall feelings of happiness and even elation.

Takeaways

- Thinking about God daily can have a profound effect on your brain and on your emotions.
- Positive and spiritual thinking changes structures in your brain.
- Meditating about God's existence can bring about feelings of joy and elation.
- Thinking about God has been shown to affect similar areas of the brain such as music and creativity.
- Meditating on God's presence may have similar effects as psychedelic drugs without any of the harmful side effects.

Questions for Self-Exploration

- Do you ever think about God?
- What happens to you emotionally when you think about God?
- What spiritual practices can you incorporate into your life?
- How would focusing on faith and trust improve your life?

CHAPTER 9:

Case Studies of Clients Whose Lives Have Changed as an Outcome of Logotherapy

"Know your potentials."
—Viktor Frankl

Logotherapy is a remarkable approach to help people who have tried countless other ways of healing depression, anxiety, or PTSD, but do not feel fully healed. They may come into therapy experiencing feelings of unhappiness, frustration, doubt, beliefs that they are a failure, or the perception of being trapped by life's circumstances. We believe that this is due to their not yet encountering their potential, inner goodness or finding more meaning in their lives.

Logotherapy provides a refreshing view of the individual who may believe that "many things are wrong with me." Instead of reaffirming and digging deeper into these beliefs, the Logotherapy clinician explores what is already right and what resources they can actualize, including values, spirituality or their inherent relationship with God.

The following transcripts are from composite sessions with my clients concerning anxiety, eczema, obesity, a broken-neck, low self-confidence and depression, procrastination, and parental burnout. The names have been changed as well as any identifying information. To enhance the reader's experience and understanding of how I conceptualize the cases and guide my clients through different levels of thinking,

I have noted in square brackets—[ ]—the values, meanings, or levels of spirituality we are accessing. I also provided an internal dialogue of the thoughts in my mind in parentheses—()—to help the reader understand the nature of my questions and comments to my clients.

Anxiety

Background: Experiencing occasional anxiety is a normal part of life. However, people with anxiety disorders frequently have intense, excessive, and persistent worry and fear about everyday situations. Often, anxiety disorders involve repeated episodes of sudden feelings of intense anxiety and fear or terror that reach a peak within minutes (panic attacks).

Miriam, a 28-year-old mother of three young children, suffered from frequent anxiety attacks. Her third child was born prematurely and spent many months in and out of the hospital. That experience triggered what Miriam described as "postpartum depression." Still reeling from the difficult birth and recovery, Miriam also had to juggle taking care of her two other young children and helping her mother, who was sick with cancer.

A year before we met, Miriam started having indigestion that worsened over time and was accompanied by dizzy spells and headaches. She had trouble sleeping and would spend many hours on her computer late at night, chatting with friends and watching movies. Before bed, she would obsess about the front door not being locked and would check it several times each night—to the dismay of her husband and children. Miriam had already been diagnosed with anxiety and was now exhibiting signs of OCD and depression.

DS: What would you like to talk about today?

Miriam: I've kind of developed a real phobia around getting into bed at night and going to sleep. I get panic attacks, really severe panic attacks when I'm just about to go to sleep.

DS: What's happening at night?

Miriam: I can't stop thinking about someone breaking in and hurting me and my children.

DS: That must be so difficult for you. What are you thinking about at night? Was there anything specific that occurred around the time when your anxieties were starting?

Miriam: Yes, I think it has to do with the birth of our third child.

DS: Yes. I'm sure there is a lot you were worried about. But what specific things were bothering you when he was born?

Miriam: We were mostly worried about our finances. You see, my husband is in a very shaky position at work. The economy is not very strong, and there is a lot of competition in his industry. He's always worried that things will not necessarily work out financially for us, and that we are going to be in trouble.

DS: Yes. I hear that you have been really scared about your future. I was just wondering: Did anything actually happen to your husband at work?

Miriam: Actually, nothing happened.

DS: You mean that he never actually lost his job?

Miriam: No he never did, but he was always stressed out that he couldn't provide for me. When we had our first two children I was working in a preschool. But after the third child, I couldn't work anymore because I had to be home with the children.

DS: So you're saying that he actually never lost his job and you have been fine.

Miriam: Yes.

DS: I'm just wondering, Miriam: Was there ever a time in your life where you were worried about something, but it didn't come true? Just slow it down and think deeply about your thoughts and see what comes up. [Beliefs]

Miriam: What's coming up is that when I was a little child my grandmother was diagnosed with breast cancer.

DS: That must've been very scary for a little girl and I'm sure you really loved your grandmother. [Values]

Miriam: I loved her very much. She was a very kind woman.

DS: So, what happened?

Miriam: She had surgery, and she eventually went into remission.

DS: What else do you remember from that time? How did your grandfather deal with it?

Miriam: My grandfather was a very optimistic personality. He always believed that everything would turn out right.

DS: How was he able to do that? [Meaning] [Values]

Miriam: I'm not sure. But I do remember hearing stories that no matter what would happen, he would only stay positive. In fact, he was a soldier in the Second World War, but he never got sent to the front. He supposedly was beloved by everyone in his unit, and was never transferred to Europe.

DS: You mean that he always had a very positive attitude, correct? [Attitude]. And where do you think he got it from? [Identity]

Miriam: I'm not sure. All I know that I heard was that when his parents were sick with rheumatoid arthritis, he got a second job just to take care of them as they got older. He was a very positive person and really cared for others. [Values]

DS: Right. He cared for others and maintained a positive attitude. Just think about that for a minute.

(Miriam starts reflecting internally and I give her a chance to process her thoughts.)

DS: How did he do that? What resources was he calling upon? Was he a religious or spiritual person? [Spirituality]

Miriam: He was a real traditionalist.

DS: He had spiritual leanings?

Miriam: He wasn't very learned, but he had a very positive attitude to religion and respected rabbinic figures.

DS: When you think about him, how do you feel?

Miriam: I have this beautiful rush of positive feelings in my chest.

DS: As you feel that, what thoughts are coming up about him? [Thoughts]

Miriam: His smile, and his positive attitude.

DS: Notice that within you. Notice his smile and his attitude. Also, maybe smile with him for a minute. [Sensations, Behaviors]

(Miriam begins to smile, and breaks out in a small laugh.)

DS: What are you feeling right now?

Miriam: Grandpa. I feel his joy.

DS: And when you think about him what happens?

Miriam: I feel happy thinking about his smile.

(A minute passes)

DS: If we could go back to that anxiety you were feeling before, how do you feel now?

Miriam: It's not so bad.

DS: Because it matters what you focus on, correct? And now, when you think about going to sleep at night, and you think about your grandfather, how do you feel? [Values, Attitude, Meaning]

Miriam: It's not as scary.

DS: Right, it's not as scary. I have a feeling that your grandfather was also channeling his relationship with God [God]. And, that had something to do with his attitude as well. What do you think?

Miriam: Now that you mention it, you're probably right. He loved going to synagogue and always had a positive attitude toward Judaism.

[Spirituality]

DS: He did, didn't he? And if he were under the same stress and situation that you're dealing with now, what would he be thinking about?

Miriam: He would probably maintain that beautiful smile and his great attitude, and connect to his spiritual beliefs.

DS: That's correct. Remember how he survived the Second World War and your grandmother's cancer. And how do you think that could help you?

Miriam: I guess if I do the same thing it would be helpful, wouldn't it? [Attitude]

DS: Yes, I think you're tapping into the right resources now to overcome this, to think about him, and to adopt his attitude. He seemed to have a lot of wisdom and loved you very much. You are very lucky to have known such a person. Let's see how you feel over the next week and how your sleep goes.

Eczema

Background: Eczema is a group of conditions that make your skin inflamed or irritated. Some people have flare-ups of the itchy rash in response to an immune system response, something irritating, or a family history of other allergies or asthma. A recent survey by the National Eczema Association revealed that more than 30% of people with atopic dermatitis were diagnosed with depression and/or anxiety. In the following session, a woman in her 50s came to speak about her lifelong battle against eczema after having a checkup with her doctor. This client came to discuss possible emotions underlying her chronic eczema, which turned into a discussion of her mother being sick throughout her childhood. She then suddenly spoke about her relationship with God and that she was created for a higher purpose. Let us take a look into the session.

DS: So, what's the problem that you're having?

Client: I have eczema, which my doctor tells me flares up when I'm under stress.

DS: Okay, how long have you had it for?

Client: It started when I was child, or somewhere around four or five. I've had periods of time in my life where it has broken out, like, all over my body. But for the past five years it's just been on my back.

DS: It's on your back . . . ?

Client: Yes, it itches sometimes but I have recently started to believe that skin problems like these are attached to emotional problems. Everything that I've gone through in fighting this disease has always been linked to stress. Whenever I changed schools or started working, it flared up. I think it was making new friends that made it worse. That's my conclusion, but I'm not sure.

DS: As you know, I'm not a doctor. And you should respect a physician's advice on this matter. However, I may be able to explore with you why you may feel so stressed at times. So together we can help you at least feel better and then we will see if that reduces your stress. So which conclusions aren't correct?

Client: I don't know, maybe all of them, not sure. I don't know, like I had it when I was young and my mom was sick. We went back and forth to my grandparents' house every week. I started fighting a lot with my older brother.

DS: What was that like when you were young, and your mom was sick?

Client: I think I just always tried to get my mother's attention and my brother was always getting in the way. I had to step down to throw tantrums and get really angry to feel seen. Also, in high school when I switched my school to another place further away, I had to fight to try to fit in. *[Beliefs]*

DS: You want to be accepted. *[Identity]*

Client: So I feel like that was a big problem for me, that's just how I operated. I believe I really got angry at myself at some point for that. I guess because I remember when I would start hanging out with the wrong crowd, I had to pretend to be someone else, when I really think about it. So, I had a lot of anger and don't know why. I dragged through my old high school and, yeah, it was very hard.

DS: Okay. So you mentioned pretending to be someone else? Who would that have been?

Client: I'm not sure.

DS: Take a moment. Who were you pretending to be in high school? [Identity]

Client: Not sure.

DS: What are you feeling now? [Behavior]

Client: I have a feeling around my chest, like a hot feeling with tingling on my hand but yeah, my right foot feels kind of heavy and then the feeling around my neck.

DS: What's that feeling in your neck?

Client: It feels like, um… like there's a cloud or like there's a stuck-ness, like it's heavy.

DS: What's happening with your neck right now?

Client: It's still like there's a darkness there. I actually feel like in my body it's a little bit uneasy. I also feel sad, but now I'm feeling angry. It's sorting through those emotions.

DS: So, what's happening now with that feeling around your neck you were feeling? [Sensation]

Client: It's not as strong. The stuck-ness, it's more of, like, a dull-like feeling. It's faint.

I still have a feeling in my left arm and a little bit around my throat, and I feel like I am still unintentionally trying to be someone that others want to see.

DS: Trying to be someone, how does that work? [Identity]

Client: It doesn't work well. I end up building resentment towards myself, towards me, because I unintentionally step into being someone that others want or I believe others want, but I don't want that.

DS: So, you don't want to be someone who you believe other people want you to be.

Client: It's like I don't want to feel like I have to be somebody that I'm not, which is not my life.

DS: So, whose life is it? [Beliefs]

Client: I don't know, but I want to be done with doing that. I've lived for years like that and I don't want to be like that again. In fact, there is no way I would ever live again like that. You couldn't pay me to try to be someone I'm not. It just creeps in like . . . I'm like . . .

DS: Like what? What is that? [Width]

Client: It's like it's my unconscious behavior. I'm thinking that I may have sabotaged years of my life.

DS: What is that doing to you?

Client: It's like a train wreck and I can't look away. I know what's happening. I step out of it. I can watch it happening, but it still happens.

DS: What's happening now? [Thoughts, Emotions]

Client: I'm remembering a thing that happened in high school. I don't want to repeat it. I also felt I couldn't be who I really am.

DS: Yes, it's your identity that you are thinking about. But you know that there are more possibilities. For example, who are you really? [Identity]

Client: I'm really good. I've always been good. No one can take that away from me. God created me. I'm a creation who God loves and created. I'm okay. [Essence]

DS: Yes you are. That's right. Makes sense, doesn't it? Take your time. Slow it down. Get in touch with thinking how good you are. Go there to find out who you are. Enjoy being there. Think about your relationship with God. [God]
(Client is quiet and introspective for around two minutes, her face softens, and she relaxes.)

DS. How are you feeling now?

Client: Better.

DS: Stay there, don't rush. You are safe within yourself. Stay in your real self. You can get this, when we just slow down.

Client: Yes, this is all settling down.

DS: What's settling down?

Client: My feelings towards myself and my identity.

DS: So, when you think about what you had to go through as a little girl back then, how do you feel about it now? [Identity]

Client: I feel detached. It's not that bad.

DS: It's actually quite good being you, the real you, isn't it?
Client: Yes, it is.

DS: Just enjoy that. Don't try to figure things out: just connect to what's really inside of you. You see, people get busy, don't they? They go through life trying to remember who they are, but it's hard. Life is tough. It tries to make you forget who you are, but you don't want that, do you?

Client: No, I don't.

DS: What do you want? [Identity] [Purpose]

Client: I want to be me.

DS: You've got it. Enjoy that right now. Enjoy being you: feeling the connection; feeling being you. No one can take that away.

Client: Yes, I'm feeling better.

DS: Better than what? [Width]

Client: Better than before. More free, open. I think I'm capable. Less stress?

DS: So, what does that have to do with your eczema?

Client: If my doctor is correct, feeling less stressed is better for my condition.

DS: That's right. It seems you were feeling stressed a lot in your life, especially when your mom was sick. [Beliefs]

Client: Oh, yes, that's probably when the stress started.

DS: Makes sense. It's really hard when you're a child watching your parent get sick. It must have been really scary. [Beliefs]

Client: Yes, it was.

DS: I mean, feeling so responsible.

Client: *(begins to cry)* Yes. It was so hard for me as a child. I felt so terribly helpless when I saw her lying in bed.

DS: How old were you then? [Identity]

Client: Around eight.

DS: Now what does that have to do with your eczema? [Beliefs]

Client: Actually, when I think back, I remember asking dad to take me to the doctor because it itched so much. He told me mom was very sick and they didn't have time to take me to the doctor.

DS: And then what happened?

Client: It got worse. So eventually I went with my aunt who was visiting from California. She took me to the doctor.

DS: Right. Just think about that for a moment. What comes up? *[Thoughts]*

Client: I felt weird that my aunt took me and not my mom! [Beliefs]

DS: That made you angry.

Client: Yes. Very.

DS: What else did you feel? *[Length]*

Client: I felt I didn't matter, and I couldn't get what I wanted.

DS: What did you want? *[Identity] [Purpose]*

Client: I wanted to be a kid. I used to be good at dance and music and my mom would take me for lessons after school.

DS: You couldn't express your talents then? *[Identity]*

Client: Right. I couldn't be a child, just playing and having fun.

DS: That's who you really were, a dancer and an artist. And you had to give that up for your mother, correct? *[Identity]*

Client: Yes, I am a dancer and artist. It's something I really love and enjoy doing. I remember—before my mother got sick—dancing and playing piano. And I enjoyed it so much. But then at some point, with mom's illness, I had to give it up and I was so upset. But I guess I just sucked it in because there's nothing I could have done.

DS: Correct, there's nothing you could have done, and it would've been nice if you were at least left to do what you enjoy doing. But from that point onwards, you seem to have focused more on your mom's needs and less on your own. Does that make sense?

Client: Yes, I think I lost myself. *[Identity]*

DS: And who is the real you?

Client: It's me, and I'm right here. *[Identity]*

DS: Right. And what is right here that was there before?

Client: Being who I am. It's my dancing, and my music. It's my relationship with God. I guess my true self is really artistic, but I had to give it up for so many years during my childhood. *[Spirituality]*

DS: You're right, I think you did, and this is also your way back to getting in touch with your higher self, the artistic and spiritual self. You see, children really are very spiritual beings, and they are very in touch with the wonders of childhood, which include dancing and music. And that spiritual part of yourself—the part where you felt at one with who you are—was put on hold for so many years. I know it's good to think about that again and get in touch with your true self. Isn't it? So, when you start feeling those sad feelings and emptiness, and even your stress, go back to music and go back to your art. *[Spirituality]*

Client: Yes I can see that, thank you so much.

Obesity

According to the Mayo Clinic, Obesity is a complex disease involving an excessive amount of body fat. Obesity is not just a cosmetic concern. It is a medical problem that increases the risk of other diseases and health problems, such as heart disease, diabetes, high blood pressure and certain cancers. There are many reasons why some people have difficulty losing weight. Usually, obesity results from inherited physiological and environmental factors as well as other emotional problems, including trauma and stress.

In the following session, a woman in her mid-forties came to speak with me about her obesity, which turned into a discussion about her guilt concerning her child's terminal illness.

DS: So, what is the problem you want to work through today?

Client: I want to lose weight.

DS: So, what would you get out of losing weight? How could your life be better?

Client: Probably wouldn't be in this much pain and could do a little bit more. I'd be healthier.

DS: Okay. So you'd be in less pain and get to do more and be healthier. That makes sense. So, what has stopped you previously?

Client: Lots of things. My job is my biggest problem. When I'm at home and I'm all alone I can't stop thinking about how my son is doing. I think I'm eating out of guilt to cover up my feelings.

DS: So, what are you covering up? *[Depth]*

145

Client: The way, I suppose, how I feel: guilty.

DS: Feelings of guilt. In connection with your weight loss? *[Beliefs]*

Client: Yeah.

DS: What else can you tell me about weight loss?

Client: I suppose, my weight, I use it to cover up hurt and guilt.

DS: Covering up hurt and guilt. *[Beliefs]*

Client: Yes.

DS: When you think about that, what comes up for you?

Client: I suppose being upset.

DS: That's right. What else? [Length]

Client: Sadness

DS: So you mentioned that you're covering up some sadness and some guilt. Can you tell me more about that? [Emotion]

Client: Well the guilt that my son has a genetic disease. What he has, even though I'm not a carrier—it was a mutant egg. So I blame myself for him and having that way.

DS: So it was your egg that was defective?

Client: Yes, I blame myself.

DS: I understand. I'm just wondering: What has that go to do with your current weight situation? [Depth]

Client: Well, I've used it as a punishment and, because of the years of caring for him, I've damaged my body as well as my back. My husband too: he has had to take on more roles and he has now got the problems that I've got as well. Then there's looking at other people our age and that they can just go out and do whatever they want.

DS: Tell me more about the guilt.

Client: Even though it wasn't genetic, it was my egg.

DS: OK, so it was your egg that was defective.

Client: Yes, right. So, I blame myself for him not having a normal life.

DS: What does guilt have to do with losing weight?

Client: I think, yeah, well, that I'm responsible. But I also know that it's probably nothing.

DS: So maybe it's probably nothing? *[Beliefs]*

Client: I'm not sure.

DS: Maybe you've turned nothing into something. What are you feeling now? *[Feelings]*

Client: Like a weight off my shoulders, like a weight off your shoulders.

DS: That's right, like weight off your shoulders. So, when nothing becomes something, you can take a weight off your shoulders.

DS: And so, how are you feeling about your relationship with your son at the moment?

Client: We have a good relationship. It's a mom thing.

DS: What's that mom thing? *[Identity]*

Client: You know, taking care of a child is a mom thing. As a mom, you always worry. You can never go away, can't go away.

DS: Because that's to do with the mom. Isn't it the worry that you could get away from?

Client: Yeah, I do. I worry that he can't have the best life that he can, right? It's just normal, normal to see what's happening there.

DS: What are you curious about?

Client: What's normal? *[Beliefs]*

DS: Wanting the best for your kids and worrying about them. [Values]

Client: Right. It's happening for wanting the best for the kids and worrying about them.

DS: Which is normal as a mom.

Client: Yep. I Know.

DS: So I wonder what we can learn from that. For yourself and for you personally. *[Beliefs]*

Client: What can we learn from that? That everything I was doing was normal.

DS: Yes. You were doing the best you could? That was your purpose, to be the best loving mom possible. That was normal, right? It was just a mom thing. *[Values]* *[Identity]*

Client: I was normal.

DS: So when you think along the terms of your weight loss journey, everything you want, everything you haven't got yet, there's something in there, isn't there?

Client: Yeah, yeah, yeah. It's just normal.

DS: So I guess everything you've done up to this point right now is normal, although you have been feeling abnormal while doing so. *Pause.*

DS: It has to have had something normal in it because you kept doing it. And I guess the good life you want for your son has to start with you, doesn't it? So, if you are living the normal life, and your son's getting the life of normalcy that you give him, it's something to be happy about, isn't it? Everybody wins. [Values] [Beliefs] [Meaning]

DS: You don't have to feel guilty about feeling it or thinking about it, canceling all that out. So how are you feeling about it right now?

Client: I'm pretty good.

DS: So, when you think about going home and being around your son, what value can you bring to him that you couldn't before? Normalcy. That's a lot to give to someone who has a child. That's the most important thing, normalcy. So, when you're feeling you are fulfilling your purpose to be the mom who gives her child normalcy, how do you feel? *[Values] [Beliefs] [Meaning] [Spirituality]*

Client: I guess that makes me feel better.

A Broken-Neck Survivor

Background: A hangman's fracture is a break in one of the vertebrae of the neck. It was made famous by the story of the actor Christopher Reeve, who fell from a horse and became a quadriplegic. In the following session, one of my students—who broke her neck in a diving accident— spoke about how she survived and what values she focused upon in order to become more resilient for her family.

DS: How can I help you?

Client: I saw online that you speak about Viktor Frankl, and I thought you could help me. Several years ago I broke my neck in a diving accident and I'm still struggling with the aftermath.

DS: What happened?

Client: I was on a family vacation in Florida, and we were there for the "Disney experience." In the evening, we were all sitting by the pool. I dove into the pool and misjudged the depth and ended up hitting the bottom of the pool with my head, then coming up from the dive with (later finding out) a "C" fracture. So, the events that followed that day were really quite traumatic, you know. Leaving my two young toddlers at the time and heading down to the hospital on day two of a two-week trip, especially in the U.S. I'm a Canadian citizen so it was also a scary experience.

A "C" fracture, for those who don't know what that means . . . Essentially, it's called the hangman's fracture, so most people end up dying immediately from that kind of break and so there were a series of events that kind of followed or transpired and I won't go into a whole bunch of details regarding them. But I was soon in a halo and it's an eight pound metal contraption where you have four pin sights in various parts of your skull for it to be stabilized, and it was to be on for days.

DS: How did you deal with that? *[Values]*

Client: I had read Viktor Frankl's book, *Man's Search for Meaning*. It was one of those books that impressed me . . . that in a dire circumstance, man's ability to get through those circumstances on the basis of perspective is quite significant.

DS: In what way? *[Length]*

Client: It helped me realize that in those difficulties there's hope and it really comes down to how you perceive the experience. [Values] [Attitude]

DS: And what else? *[Width]*

Client: Well, there are other pieces that took shape, like my faith. But overall I would say, too, that what helped me most is that I chose to concentrate on what was working, and not on what wasn't working. So, if I had some pain going on I chose to focus on the thought that I'm so lucky that I'm here for a second chance at life and I'm here to help my toddlers, you know, get up in the morning and give them breakfast. *[Values]*

DS: How were you able to do that?

Client: I was unsure at that point what was going to be at that moment. It was a very scary moment. I mean, I had my children in bed that night at home knowing they were there at the scene. . . . There were so many things that were going through my mind, and I wasn't going to be there for them in the morning the next day. I was like if they did see me in the next few days, I would look significantly different. I had compression on my spine and then on my throat so I couldn't talk very well. And it was just this realization that that was a near-death experience. In my mind I was like I can't believe that happened, and at first there was a lot of blame that I went through in terms of like, "How could I have done that?" and "How did I not judge the possibility of death?"

DS: With all this running through your mind, what did you do to survive? *[Purpose]*

Client: I guess it's that I also realized that I was still here for a reason; there was a purpose. Now, I wasn't calm, that's for sure, when I was in the hospital, and all this happened. I wasn't calm because the processing of all those things at the same time almost caused reversion to a childlike state at first. That is, until I could break it into small pieces, you know, "How am I gonna get through this once I have the halo on?" and "What am I going to say to my kids?" and "How am I going to project to them my resilience?" And I think that's the only word that I can think of in my mind that describes what I wanted to show them in my scenario. *[Purpose, Values]*

DS: Where did the resilience come from? How did you evoke that? *[Values]*

Client: Because the first time, and it's forever burnt into my mind, when my three-year-old came to see me in the hospital he was immediately in a fear-based state. You could see it all over his face. He sees his mother in a metal contraption, this halo, laying in a medical bed and trying to process what's happened. He didn't even really know what was going on, let's be real about that, and then my five-year-old just completely not knowing what to say either. And in order to help them feel comfortable at the time, the "Transformers" movie was such a big hit (this was a number of years ago) so I said to them, you know, "Mom's doing okay now." I was in a lot of pain, but I didn't tell them that. "But guess what the cool thing is? You'll be able to show me at show-and-tell to your class. I'm gonna be like a Transformer. That's what this is. It's like a metal contraption like Transformers." And then their faces softened, and they became more comfortable with the circumstance because I was trying to relate to something that would resonate with them and not thinking about how I was feeling. So putting myself in their shoes I would say that actually helped me to move forward because I wanted to show them that no matter what we go through in life it's how we deal with it that makes the difference—what we choose to focus on versus what we don't focus on makes the difference—and we have that power in ourselves to do that. *[Values] [Attitude]*

DS: Yes, that's what Viktor Frankl talks about in *"Man's Search for Meaning"* when he says that there are times in life, you're going to be facing this inescapable suffering and the only thing you could change in that moment is yourself, and you change your attitude towards a situation. He also talks about something called hyperreflection, reflecting too much in oneself. At that moment you need to start de-reflecting or reflecting on something outside of yourself. So, what values or meanings did you reflect on, beyond yourself? *[Values] [Meaning]*

Client: Yes, I mean anyone who's a parent would know this. You want to be there for your children, and you want to also show them strength at various times because they learn through us. For them more than anything I wanted to show them resiliency and how I could get through this and what strategies I would take. And it's so interesting because my oldest son, who is now turning seventeen, just wrote a paper on his traumatic experiences in his life, and one of them was seeing his mom go through this experience. But what he noted is what he learned was that he can get through anything, anything that's difficult, because of what I showed him. I'm not using his exact words but that was the essence of it. And I realized that even though they were little children at

154

the time—like five and three—it was a powerful experience for them too. DS: It seems that Viktor Frankl also thought about similar ideas. *[Values, Identity]*

Client: Yes, that's really interesting.

DS: Viktor Frankl talks about, in his books, that he was in the concentration camps and at times he was dying of typhus and knew he had to stay awake all night or die from a high fever. Or he was on a death march and his feet were swollen and he knew that if you fell you would be shot, so he imagined himself fulfilling some meaning in the future, you know, like going to teach the psychology about the concentration camps to his students. In truth he didn't know if he'd be free or alive, but he imagined that he would be free at times and would speak to his wife and share in his mind his love with her. He found out only afterwards that she was murdered in Auschwitz by the Nazis. So it seems that you too were looking at greater things than yourself at that moment to gain the strength to continue. Is that correct? *[Meaning]*

Client: Yes. I would say so for sure, and then the sense of purpose is the other component I think that comes up. And what you were just talking about is like seeing a sense of purpose beyond ourselves… when I went through this circumstance, as you can imagine, there's not a lot of people to talk to that survived this circumstance. I think the statistics are like fifty percent of individuals survive, and of that fifty percent (a small population) can walk. Most of them are para- or quadriplegic. Christopher Reeve is a good example of the hang man's fracture. And so there was no one to talk to or compare my experience with. So, I went on this mass search to find someone through the web and found Sandy Scott who lives in Florida. He was a bicycle rider that went head over tail on his bike and fractured his neck, so I started having conversations with him. And then I realized that I don't want others to go through this experience in the same way that I have. And that there are answers and there is hope. And then I set up the broken neck survivor support page on Facebook as a means to start reaching out to others and helping them through the experience. And I think now there's probably over 2,000 people there. And it's really a place where people can meet and the whole essence of it is positive reinforcement and that you do have control of what's going on in your response to the circumstance. That's the only thing that you have control of. *[Purpose] [Meaning]*

DS: Right. This is what Frankl refers to as the last of all human freedoms: to choose one's attitude. *[Attitude]*

Client: There is this grouping of people that can get into this thought process of victimization where nothing's good. And two people can have the same injury, but . . . how they choose to respond to the circumstance largely affects their outcomes. And I can see that happening because those that are like "this isn't good" or "I have so much pain" and they talk about the pain all the time, well of course the pain is going to amplify. The more you concentrate on it the worse it gets, and I know that myself because C fracture has never fused together. (So, the C is like the circular vertebrae that stabilizes your skull and the rest of your spine.) My right side is still fractured and it's worse off than it was post injury. But would you ever be able to tell by looking at me that I still have a broken neck? No! And yes I have chronic pain but I choose not to focus on that. Have I changed the way I live? No, because I don't want to live in fear so I still go skiing, I still do things that I would have done before the accident because I choose hope, I choose faith, I don't choose fear. *[Beliefs]*

DS: Very well said. Viktor Frankl says that ". . . in spite of my condition, I choose to connect to something greater than myself, something outside of myself or an experience out of myself or beyond myself." This kept him alive in Auschwitz for several years, imagining himself in situations fulfilling a meaning or loving a family member. In your case it was being there for your family and living a life in spite of your pain which kept you moving forward. *[Meaning, Values, Attitude]*

Client: Correct. Yes absolutely. I watched the video you suggested of Viktor Frankl and his student Jerry Long. I felt I was in a similar situation to him. I don't know if it was a 'C" break but he was a sportsman. I think he was going to be a baseball player or something like that and he dove, and he also broke his neck and he was a paraplegic or quadriplegic as you saw in the video. And he says he realized, not knowing much about the Holocaust, not even hearing about Viktor Frankl originally and then reading Viktor Frankl, that he was experiencing and thinking the same things that Viktor Frankl was thinking about in the camps, when he was sitting there in that bed and his whole career was finished and he's not sure he's going to live. It turns out that Jerry Long went on to do a degree in psychology and dedicated his life to helping other people who were facing inescapable suffering by changing their attitudes. The name of that video is "I broke my neck but it did not break me." *[Values]*

DS: Can you reflect on that saying for a minute, what that meant for you personally as well that it didn't break you? What value did you access to not be broken? *[Values]*

Client: I would say that the circumstance I found myself in actually taught me more about myself, more about resiliency, more about what are my values that are core to me and what are my motivators in life, and what is my purpose for being here. And all of those pieces, it almost felt like they all came together through a difficult experience. And so you know, you made mention, like my family, like that is such a huge piece for me if I can equip my kids in a way for them to realize how powerful the mind is. How powerful the mind-body connection is. Because your mind affects the response that goes on in your body and you know we have all these outside things going on around us in the world today. No doubt, there are more challenges than we see now, since we all have access to the web. But there are also more opportunities. So, my belief is if "it didn't break me," it was a gift. The experience was a gift. It was a gift in that it helped me to enrich my life and now helps me in circumstances to help others with how to get through something difficult by changing your mindset.

During the recovery I was wearing a halo around my head and neck. No one could touch me at all. Before the accident I took things for granted like hugging my children as an example. But I couldn't actually hug them and have that touch and that connection. It was one of the first things I was going to do as soon as that halo came off because I didn't realize how I took for granted some basic things that we all think we have. I mean you interact with your family every day. You hug and you say I love you but then that physical interaction when you don't have it is something that you just long for. And so, when the halo came off or they told me it was coming off, I was feeling this intense feeling of almost like *I can't wait for this freedom that I'm going to have* and *what am I going to do with that freedom*, and then also the fear that was coming into my brain too, like what does this mean for me now that the halo is coming off? Well, leading up to the halo coming off the conversation with my doctor was amazing— such a great physician. He had told me that the break was worse off than pre-halo so instead of it healing as it should have I actually had displaced way more and he said, "But we're still taking the halo off today." I was like *how could I have spent days in this halo that felt like jail and there was nothing physically that healed?* But then when it came off . . . that was some intense emotion right there. I was crying and—I just can't explain at all because it's just a moment where you're feeling freedom and fear at the same time.

DS: Did you also feel gratitude? *[Values]*

Client: Yes. I felt gratitude and the first thing that I did right after was I hugged my kids and it was just such a wonderful feeling of appreciation and gratitude for getting a second chance at life. *[Gratitude]*

DS: So did you begin to see things differently? *[Beliefs]*

Client: Yes. It's an event that has impacted most things and for me specifically. I didn't see it as a bad thing, I saw it as a good thing, in fact, because it helped me be more aware of the power that goes along with perspective. And then also in that reflection, of the times when I might have thought I was a victim in a circumstance when, all in all, reality wasn't that bad.

DS: And that's also what you learned from Frankl?

Client: Yes. That's what my mindset was and so Frankl's book . . . I talked about this at the beginning: it was so impactful to me. I remembered Viktor Frankl's book and what he went through and how he motivated himself to push through and the persistence to get through his experience and come out of it in the end. For me that was the same type of thing. You know, faith is a huge component of it too because it's a means to have a subconscious connection to something greater than yourself, and that is another piece for me. I can relate it to some imagery of when you drop a rock in the water it has ripple effects. And I didn't realize the extent of those ripple effects until now. I look back, you know, years later and I can see that there are people on the broken neck survivor support page who I've really helped. I've had people contact me and say I'm so thankful, you know, that I had someone to talk to and I realized that life gets better. [Spirituality, Faith, Values]

DS: So, a person always has a choice to make, correct?

Client: 100%. I think that that's a choice that we all have every day, in terms of gratitude and focus. If we all choose to focus on the good versus the bad, life will flow a lot better. In any way that I can support or help someone to find their light I feel like that's truly what *purpose* is: that's why we're here. You know, love your neighbor as you love yourself. And I just feel super thankful that I'm here to be able to do that. *[Values]*

Low Self-Confidence and Depression

Confidence is a feeling of trust in your abilities, qualities, and judgment. The American Psychological Association defines self-confidence as "a belief that one is capable of successfully meeting the demands of a task."

The following client struggled with self-confidence and self-love. During the session I had him focus on positive aspects of himself which turned into a discussion about his spirituality.

DS: So, what exactly do you want to work through? Give me a bit of an idea to find out what exactly it is.

Client: I'm feeling down and depressed. I feel like I lack self-confidence.

DS: I see. Are there times you don't feel as depressed or more confident? *[Exceptions]*

Client: Yes. When I do the things I like, and enjoy, I feel more confident and happier. Like when I'm playing music, I feel less depressed.

DS: Anything else?

Client: I love boating in summer and try to spend my weekends canoeing down the Delaware River.

DS: When was the last time you did that? *[Evocation]*

Client: Last summer I went canoeing with my son and his best friend.

DS: Tell me more about that. *[Length]*

Client: We had a great time. We went at the end of August when there weren't so many bugs out, and the weather was perfect. The kids had a great time portaging with the canoes from place to place and spending hours going down the river. The best part was camping at night and making a fire. We had a great time.

DS: Thinking about going down the river and having a great time, what are you noticing in your body? *[Sensation]*

Client: I'm feeling a sense of warmth in my arms, and my chest and in my heart.

DS: Excellent. Stay with that. Tell me what you notice.

Client: It feels nice, like waves of sensation.

DS: Is it happier and more confident? *[Emotion]*

Client: Yes, I would say so.

DS: So, when else are you more confident? *[Width]*

Client: While playing music.

DS: What do you play? *[Experiential Value]*

Client: Guitar.

DS: Imagine yourself playing right now.

Client: Ok

DS: What do you feel?

Client: The same feeling.

DS: Stay with that.
(The client closes his eyes and then tears up)

DS: What just happened?

Client: I started feeling something very enjoyable. It feels like something spiritual like I was praying. *[Spirituality]*

DS: Nice. What does it feel like when you're praying?

Client: I feel as if my full body gets lifted up with the music.

DS: Just continue to stay with that.

Client: It reminds me of going to shul when I was a teenager and just enjoying being with my friends.

DS: That's right. There's something very nice about being with friends, isn't that true? *[Values]*

Client: Yes

DS: Friends make you feel wanted, friends can also make you feel more confident, can't they? *[Experiential Value]*

Client: Yes, it's true.

DS: What are you feeling right now?
Client: I enjoy thinking about my friends in the shul and feeling confident.

DS: It's a spiritual experience, correct? *[Spirituality]*

Client: Yes, it is

DS: That's right. Thinking about your spirituality makes you feel more confident, doesn't it?

Client: I am confident because I am connected.

DS: That's true. Being connected makes you feel more confident, especially when you're spiritual. [Spirituality]

Client: Yes, it's like feeling confident more often and not being so hard on myself.

DS: And what stops you from doing that right now?

Client: I mean, to celebrate what I'm doing right. Yeah.

DS: So is it easier for you to focus on what you're doing wrong . . . or is it something more?

Client: Yeah. Maybe I just need a new way of thinking. Sometimes I can be positive for a while. I have to say that I'm a lot more positive now, but I've been better in the past. [Attitude]

DS: So what did you do differently then? [Exception]

Client: I focused on what I did right. [Beliefs] [Identity]

DS: When you think about focusing on your good points, what do you notice right now? *[Identity] [Exceptions]*

Client: My chest is tingling.

DS: There it is, right. So you're feeling whatever it is. I mean if we wait a bit longer it will continue to spread.

Client: It feels pleasant.

DS: Just thinking about it from a new perspective. So, what is happening now has to be less of a problem. But taking it beyond even what you wanted to feel. We naturally come up with new scenarios and new ideas. And sometimes you can just sit there thinking, you know, so you can resolve a problem and then you realize that you have the ultimate resource, the goodness within. Things become clearer. What are you noticing now? *[Spirituality]*

Client: If I think about it, I think it's not there anymore. I have already done so much in my life.
I sense knowing a lot more from this. I feel I can take on the job and I'm ready to take over. I feel so passionate. Again, I'm very passionate about it.

DS: Maybe because you were looking in the wrong place and forgetting who you really are. That's different from the person who walked in before, isn't it? *[Identity]*

Client: That's correct. It has to do with what I look at. *[Beliefs]*

DS: Yes, you really have a choice. Does that make sense?
Client: Yes. I think that's helpful.

DS: How do you feel now?

Client: Better.

DS: Better is what we are looking for. More connection to your music and your spirituality helps because you start feeling more confident when you expand that.

Client: I feel better when I'm focusing on what is spiritual and what I do right.

DS: That's right.

Procrastination

Procrastination is the act of delaying or putting off tasks until the last minute, or past their deadline. Procrastinators chronically avoid difficult tasks and may deliberately look for distractions. Procrastination tends to reflect a person's struggles with self-control.

In the following sessions, a 35-year-old woman came to speak with me about procrastination affecting finishing her degree in social work.

DS: Hi. What seems to be the problem?

Client: To be fair, I kind of know the problem, but I'm not sure how to explain it.

DS: Take a moment to think about it.

Client: So, I think it's procrastination.

DS: I understand.

Client: So, the problem is that I'm not really doing what I'm supposed to be doing, to be growing and developing my business as a social worker. So, I'm feeling afraid.

DS: And I want to understand, what is it that you may be afraid of? What are you afraid of?

Client: I don't know. Maybe: What happens if I change my career and I don't like it? *[Identity]*

DS: What's the feeling you're feeling right now?

Client: It's funny.

DS: If you could repeat that again. That sentence again.

Client: I think something's funny.

DS: What's funny?

Client: I feel like I'm stuck in the last few years when I started not liking it anymore. I just thought that my career was taking too much time in delivering and getting results. You see, my initial career wasn't really something that I had actually chosen. I started out in accounting, but I felt I had to resign. I didn't choose my career. I sort of was forced into it. *[Values] [Beliefs] [Meaning]*

DS: What happened in college when you were a student?

Client: I wanted to go to university, and I just picked a few professions that my older brother liked, like accounting. I'm like, I don't know what that means, but yeah, why not? I don't know. So, yeah, well, it was funny, I guess.

DS: So you felt forced into a field that was something you really didn't believe in?

Client: Actually, I did enjoy those two years. But I think it's because it was new. And that was a lot of learning. But now in my new career as a social worker, it's just new but different.

DS: And would it be okay for me to ask how you feel now? [Emotion]

Client: Well, I could say that life has changed for the better.

DS: Yes, it's just changed and gotten better. [Attitude]

Client: Yes, because helping others is more meaningful to me. *[Meaning]*

DS: To you, right?

Client: Yes.

DS: So, what does that have to do with your brother?

Client: I think that I have always tried to make him happy, and I still may be doing so.

DS: Right. What are you noticing right now?

Client: I don't have to live for my brother. *[Beliefs] [Meaning]*

DS: You don't, isn't that true?

Client: Yes.

DS: So, who do you have to live for? *[Beliefs, Values]*

Client: I guess myself?

DS: What do you mean? *[Depth]*

Client: What I really want is to change lives, not just manage money. *[Values] [Meaning] [Spirituality]*

DS: Why is that?

Client: Because I really enjoy helping people. [Values]

DS: So, accounting doesn't do that, does it?

Client: Not really.

DS: Maybe for your brother, his purpose was working as an accountant. To him, it was meaningful. He felt enriched by managing money. For you, it's not as meaningful. Does that make sense?

Client: Yes.

DS: I guess he wanted to share with you something he was excited about, but it wasn't for you, correct?

Client: That's right, I don't really like business.

DS: Neither do I, that's why I'm a therapist.

Client: I agree.

DS: I don't think your brother was disappointed, he just wanted you to share in his enthusiasm but that's hard for you. [Beliefs]

Client: I love him, and I don't want to disappoint him.

DS: So, what does your procrastinating about becoming a social worker have to do with that? [Depth]

Client: I guess if I move forward with my practice, deep down inside I feel that I may be disappointing him.

DS: That's right, but is that true?
Client: Maybe slightly, but not in the bigger picture.

DS: What's the bigger picture? Meaning] *[Spirituality]*

Client: Being a social worker makes a real difference in the world and changes people's lives. So that is very meaningful to me. *[Meaning]*

DS: So maybe you can tell that inner voice of guilt about disappointing your brother that you want to fulfill a different meaning than him, and that's okay.

Client: Yes, I guess you're right so it's a question of replacing my brother's needs or finding something for me.

DS: That's correct. How does that feel when you tap into what's meaningful for you?

Client: It's relieving. I feel that I can just be who I am. *[Identity]*

DS: That's what Viktor Frankl says. He believes that we become more of who we are, by fulfilling a meaning. People can only become who they were meant to be when they reach for something higher. And that something is your desire to heal people by being a social worker.

Client: It's true. I love the idea of helping others.

DS: And when you think about fulfilling a meaning, you will probably stop procrastinating, because it means so much to you. *[Meaning]*

Client: Yes. That is very helpful.

Parental Burnout

Many parents struggle to be the best parents possible. However, sometimes, despite their best efforts, they lose their temper and feel that they are total failures. Many parents also feel overwhelmed and begin to rehash their earlier disappointments and traumas with their own parents.

In the following session, a mother with several children and teenagers is overwhelmed and trying to carve out a place for herself in her family and in her career.

DS: So, what's the problem I can help you with today?

Client: I am experiencing major burnout. *[Feelings]*

DS: Tell me a little bit more about that. *[Length]*

Client: I'm a mom to three kids and I have one at home still and two out of the house. There is so much going on and I'm so tired. That is a lot and I'm tired.

DS: That's a lot and you're feeling tired.

Client: I'm feeling that I'm always failing at something, not being able to do it. I don't expect to make everybody happy. I definitely don't want to be codependent and teach my children that their happiness lies within others' happiness.

DS: So, what you're telling me, is that you do that for your children, and you tell them not to be codependent, but you don't give that opportunity to yourself. *[Depth]*

Client: Yeah yeah. I don't know why I do that. It's interesting because it's something that's been prevalent in my life for years.

DS: You've helped people for a long time.

Client: Yeah, my whole life.

DS: So, what stops you from helping yourself? *[Beliefs]*

Client: That's a good question. That's kind of something that's been new to me in the past few years. I've had resentment from about the age of six to now—I'm 38—that was not managed. Now I don't have that same resentment, I don't identify with those symptoms anymore. I still have triggers but that's no big deal. I'm learning to care for myself but I feel like a part of this is a different kind of resentment. Resentment for time lost and experience.

DS: What do you think you've missed out on? *[Beliefs]*

Client: Happiness.

DS: Happiness.

Client: It's the thing I can't give myself.

DS: You can't give yourself happiness.

Client: I listen to myself and I'm very aware of the things I know like "sleeping well" and things like that, you know… kind of returning my body to a better state on a daily basis.

DS: What are you feeling right now? *[Sensations]*

Client: A bit of numbness. I've been feeling numb which I felt like was a side effect.

DS: How does that happen?

Client: When we started speaking, I felt all this energy all over my body and then I felt numb?

DS: How do you start feeling the numbness?

Client: I thought I had an answer, but I don't, which is funny because I always have an answer.

DS: You always have an answer and now you don't.

DS: So, I wonder how that feels for somebody who always has an answer and now they don't.

Client: I don't like that feeling.

DS: You don't like that feeling. So, what's so bad about not having an answer?

Client: That's because I have tried taking care of other people and their well-being, mentally and emotionally, and that's kind of been a role I placed myself in due to childhood trauma. Like before I even started kindergarten it's like I felt like maybe there was nobody taking care of me. Nobody was taking care of me emotionally. Or nobody was taking care of my mental health, so I had to. Nobody else was gonna do that and so when I don't have an answer it feels like everything's gonna fall apart.

DS: Fall apart. What do you mean?

Client: I have lost friends in car accidents and then when I was a young adult I had a divorce, lost a home, and had to move a lot. My husband and I kind of started our relationship off really badly like the worst of the worst and should have never stayed together but now we've created something really beautiful and wonderful.

DS: So, you've created something beautiful, but you're scared of it falling apart. *[Beliefs] [Meaning] [Feelings]*

Client: I was trying to create something, and it didn't pan out. It kind of felt like I rose up from those ashes and still created something wonderful in my life. So now I guess I'm scared of letting that go. I'm scared of not, not being able to get control of, have those answers for myself, so that I can keep it all together.

DS: So you had the experience of something rising up from the ashes and rising up from devastation. *[Meaning]*

Client: It reminded me of something I told my husband the other day that I've helped him un-enmesh from his family and helped him become like a really amazing person. And now he's treating me really well and yeah that's new.

DS: So, what might you let go of? *[Beliefs]*

Client: I want to let go of the fear of losing everything or like fear of, it's because now in this year, I'm our sole income earner. I am afraid of having a husband who is depending on me being the sole income winner, I want to just live my life.

DS: Yes, live your life. In what way? *[Length]*

Client: I've been here before, I'm not afraid, but I am afraid. And it's funny because I know that I consciously know that at the same time.

What I don't know, I don't know. That's how I know I've held on to a lot and I'm finally letting the last bits of that go.

DS: You are.

Client: I don't know who I am without that.

DS: You don't know. *[Beliefs] [Identity]*

Client: To the extent you let go of all of this, and you find more of the *you* that you want, what if it's better? I guess I will be happy.

DS: Really?

Client: Well, I mean I still want to have emotions—you know I'm not definitely, like positive, you know, 100 percent of the time. So, I'm a realist and I'll understand that life has to have variations so I'm gonna doubt this as well. I don't want to carry PTSD or depression or anxiety or fear.

DS: Right, and that's what you're doing now?

Client: Yeah, they've been my friends.

DS: Sure, but who would call them their friend?

Client: Maybe. But this is exactly what I did not want to talk about and I thought I would get away with, uh, maybe an easier topic. Also, every single thing in my life has stemmed from this, right? It's not affected anything I know.

DS: I know. That feeling has come back, hasn't it?

Client: Yeah.

DS: There it is again.

Client: I'm done with this.

DS: Take your time.

Client: That's actually my goal once I feel like I'm successful. I want to pay my bills and when we're in a comfortable spot I want to buy a car for myself, and I want to pick out a car to test drive it.

DS: What's happening with the problem right now?

Client: Nothing. I guess I should just stop it.

DS: Makes sense.

Client: It's definitely new. It doesn't matter how many kids you have, with each baby it's new. It's an all new family, a new life. I don't know why I've been scared. I've been so scared of this newness. I don't feel scared of "new" now. I feel like I can embrace it and if it all goes to waste then that's on those people that made it go. I just can't just let go of trying to control it. You know in a marriage I don't control my husband and I don't control my children, don't control my parents. I don't even control my clients. There's very little in the world that's within my control other than my stuff.

DS: And your attitude, correct? [Beliefs] [Meaning]

Client: To have coping mechanisms to preserve myself, yeah, I need to get that back. That was a sense of control and I'm happy to let that go because I don't need that. Am I talking too much? Actually, I'm new, yeah.

DS: Because you've known that all along, right? The new you, the real you? One that's better.

Client: I've done that before and I've had situations where I've had to make it better for myself. My kids are older. I have lots of things to my disposal now in my 18 years of parenting and being an adult. I'm going to try to just enjoy my life, you know, let myself enjoy the colors outside and feel the breeze on my skin like all of those wonderful things that I teach my clients to kind of return their awareness to. I need to let myself do that more without guilt or any of my past coming in.

DS: Right, that's the real you, isn't it? You want something higher right? You want something that's yours, correct? [Identity] [Spirituality]

Client: Yes, thank you for saying that!

CHAPTER 10:

The "Search for Meaning" 30-Day Logotherapy Workbook

For the reader to more easily access the power of Logotherapy, whether in therapy or on their own, I've created a workbook where the ideas contained in this book can be contemplated in a series of questionnaires and worksheets.

Part A is understanding the level of meaning in your life and assessing what your values are.

Part B is the Search for Meaning 30-Day Workbook which will take you on a month-long journey to making tangible changes in your life by actualizing meaningful goals, values, and attitudes. You will be able to measure your level of meaning before and after the 30 days and notice the changes in your emotions, behaviors and overall outlook.

Part A—Establishing the Levels of Meaning in Your Life

What are your most important values?

• Authenticity	• Fun	• Religion
• Achievement	• God	• Respect
• Adventure	• Growth	• Responsibility
• Authority	• Honesty	• Security
• Autonomy	• Humor	• Self-Respect
• Balance	• Kindness	• Service
• Beauty	• Influence	• Spirituality
• Boldness	• Inner Harmony	• Stability
• Compassion	• Justice	• Trustworthiness
• Challenge	• Kindness	• Wealth
• Citizenship	• Knowledge	• Wisdom
• Community	• Leadership	• Other
• Competency	• Learning	
• Contribution	• Love	
• Creativity	• Loyalty	
• Curiosity	• Meaningful Work	
• Determination	• Openness	
• Fairness	• Optimism	
• Faith	• Patience	
• Fame	• Peace	
• Friendships	• Poise	

Choose your three top values.

_____

_____

_____

_____

Rank them in importance.

(1)_____

(2)_____

(3)_____

What has been stopping you from fulfilling your values?

_____

_____

_____

_____

What are several ways you could fulfill your values?

_____

_____

_____

_____

Meaningful Experiences

Choose three meaningful experiences that you will commit to accomplishing in the next month.

- Learn a new skill or hobby.
- Participate in a new learning experience.
- Travel to a unique destination.
- Go on a hike.
- Change your job.
- Learn a new instrument or language.
- Run a marathon.
- Write a book or article.
- Volunteer for a meaningful cause.
- Go to a local bookstore.
- Work on having a spiritual or religious experience.
- Reconnect with a friend from your childhood.
- Love someone.
- Start a new business.
- Overcome an addiction with a 12-step group.
- Go to a concert.
- Give a gift to someone for no reason.
- Go on a retreat.
- Say hello to a stranger.
- Go for therapy.
- Meditate in nature.
- Go to a waterfall.
- Other

(1)_____Target Date:_____

(2)_____Target Date:_____

(3)_____Target Date:_____

Overcoming Your Challenges

What Are You Currently Experiencing?

Close your eyes and scan your body.

What do you notice?

Where do you notice it?

What emotions are you feeling?

What thoughts are you having?

What "Thinking Traps" is your mind using?

What do you believe about yourself?

What do you believe about others?

Did your beliefs and attitudes develop from your family?

Did your beliefs and attitudes develop from trauma?

Based upon your findings, look at the chart below and decide which level of meaning you need help with. For example, is it a misplaced belief that is holding you back? If so, read the pages in the book connected to that level of meaning, and work through that chapter.

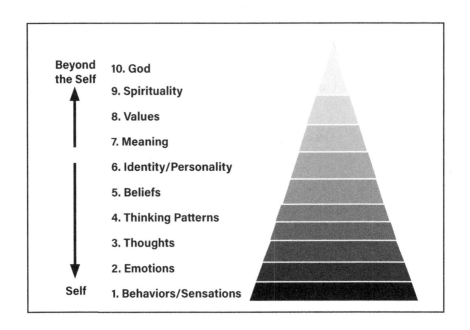

Beyond the Self

10. God

9. Spirituality

8. Values

7. Meaning

6. Identity/Personality

5. Beliefs

4. Thinking Patterns

3. Thoughts

2. Emotions

Self 1. Behaviors/Sensations

Finding more Meaning
in Your Life

1. Creative Values: (a job, vocation, hobby)

What can you do to find more meaning?

_____

_____

_____

_____

2. Experiential:

a. Who can you love, and in what ways?

_____

_____

_____

_____

b. What can you experience? (nature, music, learning, etc.)

_____

_____

_____

_____

3. Attitudinal:

Think about your attitude towards a challenge in your life (i.e. illness, financial stress, loss, etc.). What positive attitude can you choose towards it? (courage, positivity, faith, etc.)

_____

_____

_____

_____

Questions for Overcoming Suffering

Have you ever seen any good come out of a seemingly hopeless situation?

_____

_____

_____

_____

Have there been times in your life when you have been in-structed to do something you didn't want to do, but in the end found out that it was actually good for you?

_____

_____

_____

_____

Did experiencing a difficult time in your life ever make you stronger?

_____

_____

_____

_____

Using your imagination, could you write a story about how a person may experience something initially as pain-ful, but in the end it saved their life?

_____

_____

_____

_____

Is there any possible good that emerged from your own trauma?

_____

_____

_____

_____

Search for Meaning
30-Day Workbook

Take the Purpose in Life Test (PIL) found on the next page and score it. See if you are living with a high or low sense of meaning in your life.

If necessary, measure your levels of depression/anxiety.

Based on your chosen list of "meaningful activities," values, and attitudes, journal your progress over the next thirty days and then re-measure your score.

PURPOSE IN LIFE TEST (Crumbaugh & Maholick, 1964)

Instructions: Write the number (1 to 5) next to each statement that is <u>most true </u>for you right now.

SCORING: Add up all the numbers you wrote down (20-100). A score of less than 50 may indicate that you are experiencing an "existential void," a lack of meaning or purpose in your life right now...

Purpose In Life Test

1. I am usually:	bored	1 2 3 4 5	enthusiastic
2. Life to me seems:	completely routine	1 2 3 4 5	always exciting
3. In life, I have:	no goals or aims	1 2 3 4 5	clear goals and aims
4. My personal existence is:	utterly meaningless, without purpose	1 2 3 4 5	purposeful and meaningful
5. Every day is:	exactly the same	1 2 3 4 5	constantly new and different
6. If I could choose, I would:	prefer never to have been born	1 2 3 4 5	want 9 more lives just like this one
7. After retiring, I would:	loaf completely the rest of my life	1 2 3 4 5	do some of the exciting things I've always wanted
8. In achieving life goals, I've:	made no progress whatever	1 2 3 4 5	progressed to complete fulfillment
9. My life is:	empty, filled only with despair	1 2 3 4 5	running over with exciting things
10. If I should die today, I'd feel that my life has been	completely worthless	1 2 3 4 5	very worthwhile
11. In thinking of my life, I:	often wonder why I exist	1 2 3 4 5	always see reasons for being here
12. As I view the world in relation to my life, the world:	completely confuses me	1 2 3 4 5	fits meaningfully with my life
13. I am a:	very irresponsible person	1 2 3 4 5	very responsible person
14. Concerning freedom to choose, I believe humans are:	Completely bound by limitations	1 2 3 4 5	totally free to make all life choices heredity and environment
15. With regard to death, I am:	unprepared and frightened	1 2 3 4 5	prepared and unafraid
16. Regarding suicide, I have:	thought of it seriously as a way out	1 2 3 4 5	never given it a second thought
17. I regard my ability to find a purpose or mission in life as:	practically none	1 2 3 4 5	very great
18. My life is:	out of my hands and controlled by external factors	1 2 3 4 5	in my hands and I⊠m in control of it
19. Facing my daily tasks is:	a painful and boring experience	1 2 3 4 5	a source of pleasure and satisfaction
20. I have discovered:	no mission or purpose in life	1 2 3 4 5	a satisfying life purpose

Levels of Depression/Anxiety

Depression Scale

1	Minimal Depression
2	Mild Depression
3	Moderate Depression
4	Severe Depression
5	Debilitating Depression

Anxiety Scale

1	Minimal Anxiety
2	Mild Anxiety
3	Moderate Anxiety
4	Severe Anxiety
5	Debilitating Anxiety

Day 1

"Everything can be taken from a man but one thing: the last of the human freedoms—to choose one's attitude in any given set of circumstances, to choose one's own way."
—Viktor E. Frankl, *Man's Search for Meaning*

What meaningful activity/ies did you accomplish today?

_____
_____
_____
_____

What values are you committed to maintaining?

_____
_____
_____
_____

Who did you love today?

_____
_____
_____
_____

What did you experience of interest today?

_____
_____
_____
_____

What attitudes do you need to change?

_____

_____

_____

_____

Ask your future self if you are aligned with your vision and goals.

_____

_____

_____

_____

How does Frankl's quote above resonate with you on a personal level?

_____

_____

_____

_____

Day 2

"When we are no longer able to change a situation, we are challenged to change ourselves."
—Viktor E. Frankl, *Man's Search for Meaning*

What meaningful activity/ies did you accomplish today?

_____

_____

_____

_____

What values are you committed to maintaining?

_____

_____

_____

_____

Who did you love today?

_____

_____

_____

_____

What did you experience of interest today?

_____

_____

_____

_____

What attitudes do you need to change?

_____

_____

_____

_____

Ask your future self if you are aligned with your vision and goals
.

_____

_____

_____

_____

How does Frankl's quote above resonate with you on a personal level?

_____

_____

_____

_____

Day 3

"But there was no need to be ashamed of tears, for tears bore
witness that a man had the greatest of courage,
the courage to suffer."
—Viktor E. Frankl, *Man's Search for Meaning*

What meaningful activity/ies did you accomplish today?

_____

_____

_____

_____

What values are you committed to maintaining?

_____

_____

_____

_____

Who did you love today?

_____

_____

_____

_____

What did you experience of interest today?

_____
_____
_____
_____

What attitudes do you need to change?

_____
_____
_____
_____

Ask your future self if you are aligned with your vision and goals.

_____
_____
_____
_____

How does Frankl's quote above resonate with you on a personal level?

_____
_____
_____
_____

Day 4

**"An abnormal reaction to an abnormal situation
is normal behavior."
—Viktor E. Frankl,** *Man's Search for Ultimate Meaning*

What meaningful activity/ies did you accomplish today?

_____

_____

_____

_____

What values are you committed to maintaining?

_____

_____

_____

_____

Who did you love today?

_____

_____

_____

_____

What did you experience of interest today?

_____

_____

_____

_____

What attitudes do you need to change?

_____

_____

_____

_____

Ask your future self if you are aligned with your vision and goals.

_____

_____

_____

_____

How does Frankl's quote above resonate with you on a personal level?

_____

_____

_____

_____

Day 5

"Ultimately, man should not ask what the meaning of his life is, but rather must recognize that it is he who is asked. In a word, each man is questioned by life; and he can only answer to life by answering for his own life; to life he can only respond by being responsible."
—Viktor E. Frankl, *Man's Search for Meaning*

What meaningful activity/ies did you accomplish today?

_____

_____

_____

_____

What values are you committed to maintaining?

_____

_____

_____

_____

Who did you love today?

_____

_____

_____

_____

What did you experience of interest today?

_____
_____
_____
_____

What attitudes do you need to change?

_____
_____
_____
_____

Ask your future self if you are aligned with your vision and goals.

_____
_____
_____
_____

How does Frankl's quote above resonate with you on a personal level?

_____
_____
_____
_____

Day 6

**"In some ways suffering ceases to be suffering at the moment it
finds a meaning, such as the meaning of a sacrifice."
—Viktor E. Frankl,** *Man's Search for Meaning*

What meaningful activity/ies did you accomplish today?

_____

_____

_____

_____

What values are you committed to maintaining?

_____

_____

_____

_____

Who did you love today?

_____

_____

_____

_____

What did you experience of interest today?

_____

_____

_____

_____

What attitudes do you need to change?

_____

_____

_____

_____

Ask your future self if you are aligned with your vision and goals.

_____

_____

_____

_____

How does Frankl's quote above resonate with you on a personal level?

_____

_____

_____

_____

Day 7

"So, live as if you were living already for the second time and as if you had acted the first time as wrongly as you are about to act now!"
— Viktor E. Frankl, *Man's Search for Meaning*

What meaningful activity/ies did you accomplish today?

_____

_____

_____

_____

What values are you committed to maintaining?

_____

_____

_____

_____

Who did you love today?

_____

_____

_____

_____

What did you experience of interest today?

_____

_____

_____

_____

What attitudes do you need to change?

_____

_____

_____

_____

Ask your future self if you are aligned with your vision and goals.

_____

_____

_____

_____

How does Frankl's quote above resonate with you on a personal level?

_____

_____

_____

_____

Day 8

"No man should judge unless he asks himself in absolute honesty whether in a similar situation, he might not have done the same."
— **Viktor E. Frankl,** *Man's Search for Meaning*

What meaningful activity/ies did you accomplish today?

_____

_____

_____

_____

What values are you committed to maintaining?

_____

_____

_____

_____

Who did you love today?

_____

_____

_____

_____

What did you experience of interest today?

_____

_____

_____

_____

What attitudes do you need to change?

_____

_____

_____

_____

Ask your future self if you are aligned with your vision and goals.

_____

_____

_____

_____

How does Frankl's quote above resonate with you on a personal level?

_____

_____

_____

_____

Day 9

"What is to give light must endure burning."
—Viktor E. Frankl

What meaningful activity/ies did you accomplish today?

_____

_____

_____

_____

What values are you committed to maintaining?

_____

_____

_____

_____

Who did you love today?

_____

_____

_____

_____

What did you experience of interest today?

_____

_____

_____

_____

What attitudes do you need to change?

_____

_____

_____

_____

Ask your future self if you are aligned with your vision and goals.

_____

_____

_____

_____

How does Frankl's quote above resonate with you on a personal level?

_____

_____

_____

_____

Day 10

"Happiness cannot be pursued; it must ensue."
—Viktor E. Frankl, *Man's Search for Meaning*

What meaningful activity/ies did you accomplish today?

_____

_____

_____

_____

What values are you committed to maintaining?

_____

_____

_____

_____

Who did you love today?

_____

_____

_____

_____

What did you experience of interest today?

_____

_____

_____

_____

What attitudes do you need to change?

_____

_____

_____

_____

Ask your future self if you are aligned with your vision and goals.

_____

_____

_____

_____

How does Frankl's quote above resonate with you on a personal level?

_____

_____

_____

_____

Day 11

"A man who becomes conscious of the responsibility he bears
toward a human being who affectionately waits for him, or to an
unfinished work, will never be able to throw away his life.
He knows the 'why' for his existence and will
be able to bear almost any 'how.'"
— Viktor E. Frankl, *Man's Search for Meaning*

What meaningful activity/ies did you accomplish today?

_____

_____

_____

_____

What values are you committed to maintaining?

_____

_____

_____

_____

Who did you love today?

_____

_____

_____

_____

What did you experience of interest today?

_____

_____

_____

_____

What attitudes do you need to change?

_____

_____

_____

_____

Ask your future self if you are aligned with your vision and goals.

_____

_____

_____

_____

How does Frankl's quote above resonate with you on a personal level?

_____

_____

_____

_____

Day 12

"Man does not simply exist but always decides what his existence
will be, what he will become the next moment. By the same
token, every human being has the freedom to
change at any instant."
— Viktor E. Frankl, *Man's Search for Meaning*

What meaningful activity/ies did you accomplish today?

_____

_____

_____

_____

What values are you committed to maintaining?

_____

_____

_____

_____

Who did you love today?

_____

_____

_____

_____

What did you experience of interest today?

_____

_____

_____

_____

What attitudes do you need to change?

_____

_____

_____

_____

Ask your future self if you are aligned with your vision and goals.

_____

_____

_____

_____

How does Frankl's quote above resonate with you on a personal level?

_____

_____

_____

_____

Day 13

"I recommend that the Statue of Liberty on the East Coast be supplemented by a Statue of Responsibility on the West Coast."
—**Viktor E. Frankl,** *Man's Search for Meaning*

What meaningful activity/ies did you accomplish today?

_____

_____

_____

_____

What values are you committed to maintaining?

_____

_____

_____

_____

Who did you love today?

_____

_____

_____

_____

What did you experience of interest today?

_____

_____

_____

_____

What attitudes do you need to change?

_____

_____

_____

_____

Ask your future self if you are aligned with your vision and goals.

_____

_____

_____

_____

How does Frankl's quote above resonate with you on a personal level?

_____

_____

_____

_____

Day 14

**"It is not freedom from conditions, but it is freedom to take a
stand toward the conditions."**
—Viktor E. Frankl, *Man's Search for Meaning*

What meaningful activity/ies did you accomplish today?

_____

_____

_____

_____

What values are you committed to maintaining?

_____

_____

_____

_____

Who did you love today?

_____

_____

_____

_____

What did you experience of interest today?

_____

_____

_____

_____

What attitudes do you need to change?

_____

_____

_____

_____

Ask your future self if you are aligned with your vision and goals.

_____

_____

_____

_____

How does Frankl's quote above resonate with you on a personal level?

_____

_____

_____

_____

Day 15

**"For the world is in a bad state, but everything will become still
worse, unless each of us does his best."
—Viktor E. Frankl, *Man's Search for Meaning***

What meaningful activity/ies did you accomplish today?

_____

_____

_____

_____

What values are you committed to maintaining?

_____

_____

_____

_____

Who did you love today?

_____

_____

_____

_____

What did you experience of interest today?

_____
_____
_____
_____

What attitudes do you need to change?

_____
_____
_____
_____

Ask your future self if you are aligned with your vision and goals.

_____
_____
_____
_____

How does Frankl's quote above resonate with you on a personal level?

_____
_____
_____
_____

Day 16

"Everyone has his own specific vocation or mission in life;
everyone must carry out a concrete assignment that demands
fulfillment. Therein he cannot be replaced, nor can his life be
repeated. Thus, everyone's task is unique as is his
specific opportunity to implement it."
—Viktor E. Frankl, *Man's Search for Meaning*

What meaningful activity/ies did you accomplish today?

_____
_____
_____
_____

What values are you committed to maintaining?

_____
_____
_____
_____

Who did you love today?

_____
_____
_____
_____

What did you experience of interest today?

_____

_____

_____

_____

What attitudes do you need to change?

_____

_____

_____

_____

Ask your future self if you are aligned with your vision and goals.

_____

_____

_____

_____

How does Frankl's quote above resonate with you on a personal level?

_____

_____

_____

_____

Day 17

"When a person can't find a deep sense of meaning,
they distract themselves with pleasure."
—Viktor E. Frankl

What meaningful activity/ies did you accomplish today?

_____

_____

_____

_____

What values are you committed to maintaining?

_____

_____

_____

_____

Who did you love today?

_____

_____

_____

_____

What did you experience of interest today?

_____

_____

_____

_____

What attitudes do you need to change?

_____

_____

_____

_____

Ask your future self if you are aligned with your vision and goals.

_____

_____

_____

_____

How does Frankl's quote above resonate with you on a personal level?

_____

_____

_____

_____

Day 18

"If there is meaning in life at all, then there must be a meaning in suffering. Suffering is an ineradicable part of life, even as fate and death. Without suffering and death human life cannot be complete."
—Viktor E. Frankl, *Man's Search for Meaning*

What meaningful activity/ies did you accomplish today?

_____

_____

_____

_____

What values are you committed to maintaining?

_____

_____

_____

_____

Who did you love today?

_____

_____

_____

_____

What did you experience of interest today?

_____

_____

_____

_____

What attitudes do you need to change?

_____

_____

_____

_____

Ask your future self if you are aligned with your vision and goals.

_____

_____

_____

_____

How does Frankl's quote above resonate with you on a personal level?

_____

_____

_____

_____

Day 19

"We cannot, after all, judge a biography by its length, by the number of pages in it; we must judge by the richness of the contents. . . . Sometimes the 'unfinisheds' are among the most beautiful symphonies."
—Viktor E. Frankl, *The Doctor and the Soul*

What meaningful activity/ies did you accomplish today?

_____

_____

_____

_____

What values are you committed to maintaining?

_____

_____

_____

_____

Who did you love today?

_____

_____

_____

_____

What did you experience of interest today?

_____

_____

_____

_____

What attitudes do you need to change?

_____

_____

_____

_____

Ask your future self if you are aligned with your vision and goals.

_____

_____

_____

_____

How does Frankl's quote above resonate with you on a personal level?

_____

_____

_____

_____

Day 20

"Ironically enough, in the same way that fear brings to pass what one is afraid of, likewise a forced intention makes impossible what one forcibly wishes. . . . Pleasure is, and must remain, a side-effect or by-product, and is destroyed and spoiled to the degree to which it is made a goal in itself."
—Viktor E. Frankl, *Man's Search for Meaning*

What meaningful activity(ies) did you accomplish today?

_____

_____

_____

_____

What values are you committed to maintaining?

_____

_____

_____

_____

Who did you love today?

_____

_____

_____

_____

What did you experience of interest today?

_____

_____

_____

_____

What attitudes do you need to change?

_____

_____

_____

_____

Ask your future self if you are aligned with your vision and goals.

_____

_____

_____

_____

How does Frankl's quote above resonate with you on a personal level?

_____

_____

_____

_____

Day 21

"Our generation is realistic, for we have come to know man
as he really is. After all, man is that being who invented the
gas chambers of Auschwitz; however, he is also that being who
entered those gas chambers upright, with the Lord's Prayer or the
Shema Yisrael on his lips."
—Viktor E. Frankl

What meaningful activity/ies did you accomplish today?

_____

_____

_____

_____

What values are you committed to maintaining?

_____

_____

_____

_____

Who did you love today?

_____

_____

_____

_____

What did you experience of interest today?

_____

_____

_____

_____

What attitudes do you need to change?

_____

_____

_____

_____

Ask your future self if you are aligned with your vision and goals.

_____

_____

_____

_____

How does Frankl's quote above resonate with you on a personal level?

_____

_____

_____

_____

Day 22

"The meaning of life is to give life meaning."
—Viktor E. Frankl

What meaningful activity/ies did you accomplish today?

_____

_____

_____

_____

What values are you committed to maintaining?

_____

_____

_____

_____

Who did you love today?

_____

_____

_____

_____

What did you experience of interest today?

_____

_____

_____

_____

What attitudes do you need to change?

_____

_____

_____

_____

Ask your future self if you are aligned with your vision and goals.

_____

_____

_____

_____

How does Frankl's quote above resonate with you on a personal level?

_____

_____

_____

_____

Day 23

"The crowning experience of all, for the homecoming man, is the wonderful feeling that, after all he has suffered, there is nothing he need fear anymore—except his God."
—Viktor E. Frankl, *Man's Search for Meaning*

What meaningful activity/ies did you accomplish today?

_____

_____

_____

_____

What values are you committed to maintaining?

_____

_____

_____

_____

Who did you love today?

_____

_____

_____

_____

What did you experience of interest today?

_____

_____

_____

_____

What attitudes do you need to change?

_____

_____

_____

_____

Ask your future self if you are aligned with your vision and goals.

_____

_____

_____

_____

How does Frankl's quote above resonate with you on a personal level?

_____

_____

_____

_____

Day 24

"Life is not primarily a quest for pleasure, as Freud believed, or a quest for power, as Alfred Adler taught, but a quest for meaning."
—Viktor E. Frankl, *Man's Search for Meaning*

What meaningful activity/ies did you accomplish today?

_____

_____

_____

_____

What values are you committed to maintaining?

_____

_____

_____

_____

Who did you love today?

_____

_____

_____

_____

What did you experience of interest today?

_____

_____

_____

_____

What attitudes do you need to change?

_____

_____

_____

_____

Ask your future self if you are aligned with your vision and goals.

_____

_____

_____

_____

How does Frankl's quote above resonate with you on a personal level?

_____

_____

_____

_____

Day 25

"For what then matters is to bear witness to the uniquely human potential at its best, which is to transform a personal tragedy into a triumph, to turn one's predicament into a human achievement."
—Viktor E. Frankl

What meaningful activity/ies did you accomplish today?

_____

_____

_____

_____

What values are you committed to maintaining?

_____

_____

_____

_____

Who did you love today?

_____

_____

_____

_____

What did you experience of interest today?

_____

_____

_____

_____

What attitudes do you need to change?

_____

_____

_____

_____

Ask your future self if you are aligned with your vision and goals.

_____

_____

_____

_____

How does Frankl's quote above resonate with you on a personal level?

_____

_____

_____

_____

Day 26

"Man is capable of changing the world for the better if possible, and of changing himself for the better if necessary."
—Viktor E. Frankl, *Man's Search for Meaning*

What meaningful activity/ies did you accomplish today?

_____

_____

_____

_____

What values are you committed to maintaining?

_____

_____

_____

_____

Who did you love today?

_____

_____

_____

_____

What did you experience of interest today?

_____

_____

_____

_____

What attitudes do you need to change?

_____

_____

_____

_____

Ask your future self if you are aligned with your vision and goals.

_____

_____

_____

_____

How does Frankl's quote above resonate with you on a personal level?

_____

_____

_____

_____

Day 27

**"It is a peculiarity of man that he can only live by
looking to the future."
—Viktor E. Frankl, *Man's Search for Meaning***

What meaningful activity/ies did you accomplish today?

_____

_____

_____

_____

What values are you committed to maintaining?

_____

_____

_____

_____

Who did you love today?

_____

_____

_____

_____

What did you experience of interest today?

_____

_____

_____

_____

What attitudes do you need to change?

_____

_____

_____

_____

Ask your future self if you are aligned with your vision and goals.

_____

_____

_____

_____

How does Frankl's quote above resonate with you on a personal level?

_____

_____

_____

_____

Day 28

"Man is not fully conditioned and determined but rather determines himself whether he gives in to conditions or stands up to them."
—Viktor E. Frankl

What meaningful activity/ies did you accomplish today?

_____

_____

_____

_____

What values are you committed to maintaining?

_____

_____

_____

_____

Who did you love today?

_____

_____

_____

_____

What did you experience of interest today?

_____

_____

_____

_____

What attitudes do you need to change?

_____

_____

_____

_____

Ask your future self if you are aligned with your vision and goals.

_____

_____

_____

_____

How does Frankl's quote above resonate with you on a personal level?

_____

_____

_____

_____

Day 29

"The more one forgets himself—by giving himself to a cause to serve or another person to love—the more human he is and the more he actualizes himself."
—Viktor E. Frankl, *Man's Search for Meaning*

What meaningful activity/ies did you accomplish today?

_____

_____

_____

_____

What values are you committed to maintaining?

_____

_____

_____

_____

Who did you love today?

_____

_____

_____

_____

What did you experience of interest today?

_____

_____

_____

_____

What attitudes do you need to change?

_____

_____

_____

_____

Ask your future self if you are aligned with your vision and goals.

_____

_____

_____

_____

How does Frankl's quote above resonate with you on a personal level?

_____

_____

_____

_____

Day 30

"What man actually needs is not a tensionless state but rather the striving and struggling for a worthwhile goal, a freely chosen task. What he needs is not the discharge of tension at any cost but the call of a potential meaning waiting to be fulfilled by him."
—Viktor E. Frankl

What meaningful activity/ies did you accomplish today?

_____

_____

_____

_____

What values are you committed to maintaining?

_____

_____

_____

_____

Who did you love today?

_____

_____

_____

_____

What did you experience of interest today?

_____

_____

_____

_____

What attitudes do you need to change?

_____

_____

_____

_____

Ask your future self if you are aligned with your vision and goals.

_____

_____

_____

_____

How does Frankl's quote above resonate with you on a personal level?

_____

_____

_____

_____

**After 30 days of journaling, retake the PIL Test and
measure your levels of depression/anxiety**

Purpose in life test

1. I am usually:	bored	1 2 3 4 5	enthusiastic
2. Life to me seems:	completely routine	1 2 3 4 5	always exciting
3. In life, I have:	no goals or aims	1 2 3 4 5	clear goals and aims
4. My personal existence is:	utterly meaningless, without purpose	1 2 3 4 5	purposeful and meaningful
5. Every day is:	exactly the same	1 2 3 4 5	constantly new and different
6. If I could choose, I would:	prefer never to have been born	1 2 3 4 5	want 9 more lives just like this one
7. After retiring, I would:	loaf completely the rest of my life	1 2 3 4 5	do some of the exciting things I've always wanted
8. In achieving life goals, I've:	made no progress whatever	1 2 3 4 5	progressed to complete fulfillment
9. My life is:	empty, filled only with despair	1 2 3 4 5	running over with exciting things
10. If I should die today, I'd feel that my life has been	completely worthless	1 2 3 4 5	very worthwhile
11. In thinking of my life, I:	often wonder why I exist	1 2 3 4 5	always see reasons for being here
12. As I view the world in relation to my life, the world:	completely confuses me	1 2 3 4 5	fits meaningfully with my life
13. I am a:	very irresponsible person	1 2 3 4 5	very responsible person
14. Concerning freedom to choose, I believe humans are:	Completely bound by limitations	1 2 3 4 5	totally free to make all life choices heredity and environment
15. With regard to death, I am:	unprepared and frightened	1 2 3 4 5	prepared and unafraid
16. Regarding suicide, I have:	thought of it seriously as a way out	1 2 3 4 5	never given it a second thought
17. I regard my ability to find a purpose or mission in life as:	practically none	1 2 3 4 5	very great
18. My life is:	out of my hands and controlled by external factors	1 2 3 4 5	in my hands and I☒m in control of it
19. Facing my daily tasks is:	a painful and boring experience	1 2 3 4 5	a source of pleasure and satisfaction
20. I have discovered:	no mission or purpose in life	1 2 3 4 5	a satisfying life purpose

Depression Scale

1	Minimal Depression
2	Mild Depression
3	Moderate Depression
4	Severe Depression
5	Debilitating Depression

Anxiety Scale

1	Minimal Anxiety
2	Mild Anxiety
3	Moderate Anxiety
4	Severe Anxiety
5	Debilitating Anxiety

Compare the scores from the PIL and the depression/anxiety tests before and after the 30 days.

	Before 30 days of journaling	After 30 days of journaling
PIL Test score		
Depression score		
Anxiety score		

Acknowledgments

Writing a book is no small endeavor, especially when you care so much about the topic, and you want to make sure that the reader understands and can utilize the concepts you are presenting in their entirety. A work of this nature also requires significant support from people around you, including friends, families, colleagues, students, and clients who provide us with the inspiration to do the work we do.

First and foremost, I would like to thank my wife Daniella for being there with me during the entire project. During those long hours where I wrote late into the night, she was right there behind me. Knowing about my interest in promoting the ideas of Viktor Frankl, she understood that the content I was creating and the messages within the book were going to make a significant impact on countless clients and individuals seeking wisdom and counsel in the field of therapy and spirituality. Without her support nothing would have been done.

I have great appreciation towards Rabbi Benyamin Walters who carefully reviewed my chapter on the Mitteler Rebbe making the translation of concepts as accurate as possible. I would also like to thank Talia Weiner, a graduate student at the Department of Marriage and Family Therapy at Yeshiva University, for editing the book and giving it a more contemporary voice that can speak to a new generation of young and budding therapists. Her endeavors have made a qualitative difference in the presentation of my ideas.

Finally, when I've been asked in the past about who I would like to meet in history, I often answered "Moses, the Rambam, the Maharal, the Alter Rebbe, Rabbi Dovber (the Mitteler Rebbe), *and* Viktor Frankl." Although I never had the opportunity to meet or study under Viktor Frankl, I would like to express tremendous gratitude to him, in his memory, for his work and for his life. It is no easy task to go in the opposite direction of psychotherapy, which progressively focused on the exploration of the "self," and instead to ask his clients to search for meaning. But today, it is obvious that he was correct that the greatest challenge facing humanity *is* the existential vacuum experienced so persuasively in the Western world.

Perhaps the meaning of Frankl's suffering was for the benefit of countless students and individuals in the future who would now listen to his voice and be inspired by his teachings. Who knows whether he would have had the same impact if not for the tragedies that befell him, and for his heroic efforts to find meaning in spite of the suffering he endured during the Holocaust.

For me, the greatness of Frankl was that instead of falling into despair, he returned to Vienna after the war and fought a lifelong battle to have the world around him hear the "unheard cry" for meaning. I am greatly indebted to him, his ideas, and the legacy he left behind. I hope he would have appreciated my efforts.

References

Quote

1. Jacobson, Y. Y. (2011, February 1). "The Rebbe and Viktor Frankl – Part 2," *Algemeiner.com*. Accessed Jan. 13, 2024 from https://www.algemeiner.com/2010/06/25/the-rebbe-and-viktor-frankl/

Introduction

1. Frankl, V. E. (1969). *The Will to Meaning. Foundations and Applications of Logotherapy.* New York: Meridian), p. 23
2. Fabry, J, Bulka, R., Sahakian, W. (1979). *Logotherapy in Action.* (New York: Aronson), p. x

Chapter 1

1. Frankl, V. (1975). *The Unconscious God: Psychotherapy and Theology.* (New York: Simon and Schuster), p. 42
2. Freud, S. (1927). *The Future of an Illusion.* (New York: W. W. Norton and Company), p. 39
3. Wehrenberg, Margaret (2014). "Cure or Control: Depression as a Chronic Condition," *Psychotherapy Networker,* November/

December 2014. Excerpt accessed Jan. 13, 2024 from https://www.
psychotherapynetworker.org/article/cure-or-control/

4. Schonbuch, D. (2016). *Think Good and It Will Be Good: Spiritually-Based Therapy Inspired by Viktor Frankl and Jewish Wisdom.* (New York: Simon Aron Publishers)

Chapter 2

1. Frankl, V. (1975). *The Unconscious God: Psychotherapy and Theology* (New York: Simon and Schuster), p. 10

2. de Shazer, S. (1988). *Clues: Investigating Solutions in Brief Therapy*, ed. edition. (New York: W. W. Norton & Company), p. 4

3. *Psychology Now* (YouTube channel). (November 22, 2021). "Rare Interview with Viktor Frankl 1977" [Video]. https://www.youtube.com/watch?v=o4uAsVvtqIQ

4. *Levan Ramishvili* (YouTube channel). (January 3, 2017). "Viktor Frankl on Why Idealists Are Real Realists" https://www.youtube.com/watch?v=loay2imHq5E

5. Frankl, V. (1963). *Man's Search for Meaning.* New York: Simon and Schuster, p. 127

6. Hurwitz, Y., "Breaking Through a Dark Place in Your Life." Accessed Jan. 13, 2024 from https://www.chabad.org/holidays/chanukah/article_cdo/aid/4675330/jewish/Breaking-Through-a-Dark-Place-in-Your-Life.htm

7. Frankl, V. (1963). *Man's Search for Meaning*, op. cit., pp. 86–87 and 127,

8. *Viktor Frankl Fan Club* (YouTube Channel) (n.d.). Jerry Long: "I Broke My Neck, -but It Did Not Break Me" [6:55]. Accessed Jan. 13, 2024 from https://www.youtube.com/watch?v=Xx_s88bcJ_0

9. Long, Jerry (1988). Viktor Frankl Institute Promotional Award Biography, 2000. Accessed Jan. 13, 2024 from https://www.viktor-frankl.org/cvE_long.html

Chapter 3

1. *Schonbuch, D.: Torah Psychology* (YouTube Channel) (October 3, 2021). "Viktor Frankl, The Holocaust and a Broken Neck: Vanessa Chesters speaks to Daniel Schonbuch*"* [Video]. YouTube. Accessed Jan. 13, 2024 from https://www.youtube.com/watch?v=1JakM3ClifM

2. Beck, J. (2021). *Cognitive Behavior Therapy: Basics and Beyond,* Third Edition. (New York: The Guilford Press), p. 33

3. *Anxiety Canada* (2020). "Thinking Traps." Accessed Jan. 14, 2024 from https://www.anxietycanada.com/sites/default/files/ThinkingTraps.pdf

4. Fabry, J. (1968). *The Pursuit of Meaning.* (New York: Beacon Press).

5. Ryan, W. (2019). "Viktor Frankl: Philosophical Themes in Logotherapy." *UTP Journals,* Volume 36, Issues 1–2, March–June 2013, published 2019, pp. 47–63. Accessed Jan. 14, 2024, from https://www.utpjournals.press/doi/full/10.3138/uram.36.1-2.47

6. Frankl, V. (1970). *The Will to Meaning.* (New York: Meridian Books), p. 70

Chapter 4

1. *iakhan90* (YouTube channel). (October 28, 2011). "Finding Meaning in Difficult Times (Interview with Dr. Viktor Frankl)*"* 2:40. Accessed Jan. 15, 2024, https://www.youtube.com/watch?v=LlC2OdnhIiQ

2. Frankl, V. (1963). *Man's Search for Meaning.* (New York: Simon and Schuster), pp. 127 and 178

3. Rabbi Shneur Zalman of Liadi (1848). *Likutei Torah, Parshat Vayikra.* Accessed Jan. 29, 2024, from https://files.anash.org/uploads/2021/03/Pesach-maamar.pdf

4. Ibid., p. 182

5. Rabbi Shneur Zalman of Liadi (1796), *Tanya, Likutei Amarim: Sefer Shel Beinonim.* (Brooklyn, N.Y.: Kehot Publication Society), Chapter 2

6. Frankl, V. (1975). *The Unconscious God: Psychotherapy and Theology.* (New York: Simon and Schuster), p. 12

7. Ibid.

8. Ibid., p. 42

9. *Cteener* (YouTube channel) (February 25, 2019). "I'm Yitzi Hurwitz, And I Know That I Matter," Accessed Jan. 14, 2024, https://www.youtube.com/watch?v=JS12O1ndM5g

10. Ibid.

Chapter 5

1. Frankl, V. (1963). *Man's Search for Meaning.* (New York: Simon and Schuster), pp. 127 and 194–195

2. "Pursuit of Happiness: Viktor Frankl." Accessed Jan. 14, 2024 from https://www.pursuit-of-happiness.org/history-of-happiness/viktor-frankl/

3. Frankl, V. (1963). *Man's Search for Meaning.* (New York: Simon and Schuster), pp. 59 and 127.

5. Markel, Rabbi A. (tr.) (2010). *Divine Inspiration: Kuntres Hitpaalut* by Rabbi Dovber of Lubavitch. Accessed Jan. 14, 2024, from http://truekabbalah.com/docs/Kuntras_HaHitpaalut.pdf

5. Ibid., p. 32

6. Ibid., p. 25

7. Ibid., p. 32

8. Ibid., p. 33

9. Ibid., p. 34

10. Ibid., p. 35

11. Ibid., p. 36

12. Ibid., p. 39

13. Ibid., p. 28

14. Geralyn Dexter, PhD, LMHC, "What Is Systematic Desensitization Therapy and How Does It Work?" Accessed March 20, 2024, from https://www.verywellhealth.com/systematic-desensitization-5214330#:~:text=Systematic%20desensitization%20is%20a%20type%20of%20behavioral%20treatment.

15. Cocchimiglio, S. (April 11, 2022). "What Is Paradoxical Intention Therapy Used For?" Accessed March 20, 2024, from https://www.betterhelp.com/advice/therapy/paradoxical-intention-how-it-works/

16. Frankl, V. (1963). *Man's Search for Meaning.* (New York: Simon and Schuster), pp. 63–64 and 127

Chapter 6

1. Markel, Rabbi A. (tr.) (2010). *The Gate of Unity* [Translation and adaptation into English of *Shaar HaYichud VeHaEmunah* by Rabbi Dovber of Lubavitch]. Accessed Jan. 14, 2024, from http://truekabbalah.com/wp-content/uploads/2021/05/The-Gate-of-Unity-Volume-1-Second-Edition.pdf. p. 11

2. Ibid., p. 12

3. Beck, L. A. (1992). Csikszentmihalyi, Mihaly. (1990). "Flow: The Psychology of Optimal Experience [book review]." *Journal of Leisure Research*, 24(1), 93–94. Accessed Jan. 14, 2024, from https://www.tandfonline.com/doi/abs/10.1080/00222216.1992.11969876

4. Markel, Rabbi A. (tr.) (2010). *The Gate of Unity.* Translation and adaptation into English of *Shaar HaYichud VeHaEmunah* by Rabbi Dovber of Lubavitch. Accessed Jan. 14, 2024, from http://truekabbalah.com/wp-content/uploads/2021/05/The-Gate-of-Unity-Volume-1-Second-Edition.pdf p. 14

5. Ibid., p. 14.

Chapter 7

1. Fredrickson, B. (2009). *Positivity: Top-Notch Research Reveals the 3-to-1 Ratio That Will Change Your Life.* (New York: Crown), p. 217

Chapter 8

1. Rosmarin, D. H., Pargament, K. I., Pirutinsky, S., Mahoney, A. (2010). "A Randomized Controlled Evaluation of a Spiritually Integrated Treatment for Subclinical Anxiety in the Jewish Community, Delivered via the Internet." *Journal of Anxiety Disorders* (Oct. 24, 2010) (7):799–808. doi: 10.1016/j.janxdis.2010.05.014. Epub Jun. 9, 2010. PMID: 20591614. Accessed Jan. 14, 2024, from https://pubmed.ncbi.nlm.nih.gov/20591614/

2. Riken Research, "The power of positive memories." Accessed on Jan. 15, 2024, from http://www.riken.jp/en/research/rikenresearch/highlights/8088/.

3. Perreau-Linck, E.; Beauregard, M.; Gravel, P.; Paquette, V.; Soucy, J.; Diksic, M.; and Benkelfat, C. (2007). "In Vivo Measurements of Brain Trapping of C-labelled Alpha-methyl-L-tryptophan during Acute Changes in Mood States." *Journal of Psychiatry and Neuroscience* 32 (6).

4. Patel, Lyla (2020). "Video Games on the Brain." Accessed on Jan. 15, 2024, from https://scholarblogs.emory.edu/artsbrain/author/lnpatel/

5. Beauregard, M. & Paquette, V. (2006). "Neural Correlates of a Mystical Experience in Carmelite Nuns." *Neuroscience Letters*, 405. 186–190 (2006). Accessed on Jan. 15, 2024, from https://institutpsychoneuro.com/wp-content/uploads/2015/08/Beauregard2006-Carmelites-fmri.pdf

6. Newberg, A., Newberg, A. B., & Waldman, M. R. (2009). *How God Changes Your Brain: Breakthrough Findings from a Leading Neuroscientist.* (Ballantine Books), p. 7; and Pourdehnad, M., Alavi, A., d'Aquili, E. G. "Cerebral Blood Flow during Meditative Prayer: Preliminary Findings and Methodological Issues." *Perceptual and Motor Skills.* Oct. 2003; 97(2):625–30. doi: 10.2466/pms.2003.97.2.625. PMID: 14620252.

7. Newberg, A., Alavi, A., Baime, M., Pourdehnad, M., Santanna, J., d'Aquili, E. G. "The Measurement of Regional Cerebral Blood Flow during the Complex Cognitive Task of Meditation: A Preliminary SPECT Study." *Psychiatry Research.* Apr. 10, 2001; 106(2):113–22. doi: 10.1016/s0925-4927(01)00074-9. PMID: 11306250.

8. Ibid.

9. Newberg, A. B., & Waldman, M. R. (2009). *How God Changes Your Brain: Breakthrough Findings From a Leading Neuroscientist.* (New York: Ballantine Books), p. 124

10. Ibid., p. 55

11. Ibid., p. 56

12. *NPR: Talk of the Nation* (2010). "Neurotheology: This Is Your Brain on Religion."Accessed on Jan. 15, 2024 from https://www.npr.org/2010/12/15/132078267/neurotheology-where-religion-and-science-collide

13. Ferguson, M. A., Nielsen, J. A., King, J. B., Li Dai, Giangrasso, D. M., Holman, R., Korenberg, J. R., & Anderson, J. S. (2018) "Reward, Salience, and Attentional Networks Are Activated by Religious Experience in Devout Mormons." *Social Neuroscience,* 13:1, 104–116, DOI: 10.1080/17470919.2016.1257437 Accessed on Jan. 16, 2024 from https://www.tandfonline.com/doi/citedby/10.1080/17470919.2016.1257437?scroll=top&needAccess=true

Index

About the Author

Rabbi Daniel Schonbuch, LMFT, is a distinguished therapist, author, and expert in the integration of psychological and spiritual principles for emotional wellness. With a master's degree in Marriage and Family Therapy, Rabbi Schonbuch has dedicated his career to helping individuals and families navigate the complexities of mental health, relationships, and personal growth.

His unique approach combines decades of clinical experience with deep spiritual wisdom, drawing from both contemporary therapeutic techniques and timeless teachings from Jewish tradition.

Rabbi Schonbuch is a leading advocate for the use of Viktor Frankl's logotherapy, emphasizing the critical role of meaning in achieving emotional and mental health. He is the author of several influential books, including *Think Good and It Will Be Good: Spiritually-Based Therapy Inspired by Viktor Frankl and Jewish Wisdom*, which explores the intersection of cognitive-behavioral therapy and spiritual growth.

In addition to his private practice, Rabbi Schonbuch is a sought-after speaker and educator, offering workshops and seminars on logotherapy, spiritual resilience, and emotional wellness. He has trained many therapists and mental health professionals in his integrative approach, impacting the lives of individuals and communities around the world. For more, visit torahpsychology.org.

Made in the USA
Las Vegas, NV
02 January 2025

15758189R00164